Susan,

All The Best!

Jim Welsh

GROW NOW

8 Essential Steps to **FLEX** your Leadership Muscles

by **Jim Welch** with Bill Althaus

HENCHARD PRESS LTD.

Henchard Press, Ltd

Publisher	Henry S. Beers
Associate Publisher	Richard J. Hutto
Associate Publisher	Rick L. Nolte
Executive Vice President	Robert G. Aldrich
Operations Manager	Gary G. Pulliam
Editor-in-Chief	Joni Woolf
Art Director/Designer	Julianne Gleaton
Designer	Daniel Emerson
Director of Marketing and Public Relations	Mary D. Robinson
Distribution	Nick Malloy

Printed in the USA.
10 9 8 7 6 5 4 3 2 1

Library of Congress Control Number: 2007934432

ISBN: (13 digit) 978-1-934144-02-2
       (10 digit) 1-934144-0209

Henchard Press books are available at quantity discounts with bulk purchase for educational, business, or sales promotional use. For information, please write to:
Henchard Press Ltd., SunTrust Bank Building, 435 Second Street,
Suite 320, Macon, GA 31201, or call 866-311-9578.

DEDICATION

This is a special dedication to Christine Welch who collaborated with us along every step of the journey.

ACKNOWLEDGMENTS

A very special acknowledgment to my wife, Christine and my sons, Jeff and Mike Welch.

A very special acknowledgment to the Althaus family, including Bill's wife, Stacy and his sons, Zach and Sean.

Thanks also to my mentors and associates, John Beeder, Teri Brown, Jay Dittmann, Don Fletcher, Carol Hallquist, Jolee Mason, Brad Moore, Steve Paoletti, Doug Porter, Greg Raymond, Letha Steffey, Ira Stolzer, Wayne Strickland and John Sullivan who have all taught me the true meaning of bringing passion and energy to work every day.

I also wish to thank and acknowledge Steve Gardner, CEO of Five Star Speakers, who is a great coach and friend.

Bill and I also want to acknowledge Bob Snodgrass, a tremendous partner who worked closely with us every step of the way.

CONTENTS

"The truth is – Practical Growth Leaders are **made**, not born."

INTRODUCTION

The writing style I utilize in this book is consistent with the way I speak in front of audiences who want to learn how they can become Practical Growth Leaders. Critical leadership concepts are combined and explained by utilizing pop culture, movie, music and sports references. I do this to help the audience relate to my concepts in ways that are powerful, entertaining and memorable.

So, are you ready to learn what it takes to flex your leadership muscles to grow your business? If you are, I promise you won't have to step into a gym or lift a single weight. Do you have what it takes to become a Practical Growth Leader? Sure you do! The truth is – Practical Growth Leaders are made, not born.

Comedian Jerry Seinfeld once said, "A bookstore is one of the only pieces of evidence we have that people are still thinking." Are you ready to go on a fun ride that involves thinking, learning and doing? Each chapter of this book represents a critical step along the way. The journey will be fun, challenging and rewarding. You will need to pass a test hurdle at the end of each step in order to progress to the next level. You will also be given a separate implementation exercise plan at the end of each chapter where you can flex your leadership muscles on a step-by-step basis. Think of it like the NCAA basketball tournament. The goal is to advance to the next round. Will you be UCLA's John Wooden, the winningest coach in the history of the tournament and a coach whose team always seemed to peak at the right time of the year, or the coach whose overconfident team goes into the tourney with a full head of steam, only to see an underdog squad knock them out of contention? We're going to show you how to avoid the upsets and become a perennial winner like Wooden, who once said, "Remember, it's what you learn after you know it all that counts."

How do you effectively grow your business? At the end of the day, you first must create a growth culture, with the best leaders to build a sustainable model. Second, you must find ways to leverage growth starters such as innovation and customer loyalty to effectively drive your business. Finally, you must find ways to keep the momentum going every day to pursue growing your business with a passion. The 8-step model in this book provides you with the roadmap and the practical tools you will need to make these things happen.

The 8 steps are interlocking and interdependent. Before you do anything else, you must first flex the Practical Growth Leadership Culture Machine

(Step 1). Remember that haunting voice from "Field of Dreams," that told an Iowa corn farmer, "If you build it, they will come?" Well, if you build this Growth Culture Machine, you'll have so many pleased customers as well as loyal employees you'll feel like you just hit a grand slam homer and pulled off the shopping bargain of the new millennium at the same time! If you fail to flex your Leadership Culture Machine successfully, the remaining 7 steps no longer matter.

Once you flex the Growth Culture Machine, you must be able to begin refueling your growth engines by winning the battle for top talent. (Step 2). If you fail to recruit and retain the very best people, your company will not grow. It is that simple. Don't be the driver who takes a chance on the final lap of the race only to run out of fuel as your opponent sails past you to take the checkered flag. If you do not win the battle for top talent, this will likely happen to you.

This is followed by Put the Pedal to the Metal of Customer Loyalty Now (Step 3). There is no growth driver more important than increasing customer loyalty. It will help you to protect and solidify your customer base. Another critical growth driver is flexing your Innovation Flight Plans (Step 4). Innovation that creates new products, services and business improvements, within and adjacent to your core business, is the high-octane fuel of the Practical Growth Leader. Then, you will learn how to leverage key points of competitive advantage with your customers by finding the Fast Passing Zones to finish first (Step 5). Fast Passing Zones where you can move ahead of your competitors by leveraging key strengths against their weaknesses are very important to growing the business. This will be followed by learning how to stay focused on growth by successfully Building the Growth Curves of your company (Step 6). The growth curve concept which will be described in Chapter 6 will share the key leadership characteristics needed to embrace growth, and never accept a permanent position as a stagnant or declining business. A key enabler for you to win and grow consistently is to learn how to go Speeding with Your Strengths every day (Step 7). The faster pace of change combined with higher customer expectations have made speed a key ingredient in the growth race. Finally, you will learn how to Adjust Your Sails around the reefs and construction zones that stand between you and your team achieving your growth objectives (Step 8). These show stoppers can slow down and even kill growth. We will show you what they are and share ideas on how to avoid them along your successful journey to "GROW NOW!"

We will also show you how to combine all 8 essential steps of this journey and how they can be integrated with key connection points to grow your business (Chapter 9). The real strength of this model is ignited when you leverage all 8 essential steps together operationally to run your business. Finally, we will provide a specific plan to sustain flexing your growth leadership muscles every day to keep the momentum going forward (Chapter 10).

You will be tested at the end of each step to make sure you clear the hurdle to move on to the next chapter. You will also be given a 90-day flex plan to apply each step specifically to your business. These growth flex plans at the end of each step provide a roadmap to lead the changes necessary to achieve your objectives. This is not a book that involves just thinking of new ways to drive business growth. It is also a practical growth book about implementing new leadership strategies in a different and exciting way to achieve your growth goals.

As Hank Williams Jr. asked on Monday nights, "Are you ready for some football?" Now is the time to ask yourself: Are you ready for some real growth? As you begin this journey, you must conquer your fears about the risks associated with real and sustainable growth leadership. Oprah Winfrey said, "Whatever you fear most has no power...it is your fear that has the power." After you complete this journey, you will be fearless. Remember, fear is the number one enemy of growth.

Vince Lombardi, the iron-jawed former head coach of the Green Bay Packers, once growled to his team, "Winning isn't everything, it's the only thing." When it comes to growth, culture isn't everything, it's the only thing. There is nothing more important to generating sustainable growth than the culture created by your leaders. If you and your team commit to growth and take the journey through the 8 challenging steps to flex your growth leadership muscles, your culture (large or small) will never be the same. Like Lombardi's Packers, you will simply be known as the best of the best.

If you are looking for a reference guide or a few powerful ideas about Practical Growth Leaders, put this book down and go do something else. This is a model that builds over 8 defined steps that are interdependent and interlocking in their relationship with each other. If you are unsuccessful with Step 4, steps 5 through 8 no longer matter. The model is literally like building a house from the foundation to the chimney. If you're thinking about the tiles on the roof and the basement isn't finished, you're reading the wrong book. The good news is that this model and process can be successfully migrated and virally exported throughout your company to create real growth. Zig Ziglar said, "You need a plan to build a house. To build a life, it is even more important to have a plan or goal." The same is true in growing a business.

The other critical principle of this book is that this 8-step model works for companies of all sizes. Are you David or Goliath? Do you have the corner office, or do you sit in a cubicle that barely has room for a computer, a chair and you? It doesn't matter. I can say with great pride that I sat in both places along the growth journey. There are a number of critical business approaches in the marketplace today that highlight the differences between small and large companies. These differences are real. However, in my opinion, real leadership leverage can be found by focusing on the similarities rather than the differences. The leverage is effectively applied with an 8-step integrated growth leadership model that can be applied successfully across industries and organizations of all different shapes and sizes. As you migrate from one career choice to another, the model fits well into your briefcase or backpack and will help you win in each new role along your journey.

We will build the 8 steps to flex your Practical Growth Leadership muscles together. You will now go on a journey to change your Growth Leadership Culture, win the battle for talent, build customer loyalty, Flex Your Innovation Flight Plans, find the Fast Passing Zones, successfully Build the Growth Curves, Speed with Your Strengths and Adjust Your Sails to finish first.

Are you and your team ready to take the 8 essential steps to Flex Your Leadership Muscles? If so, then buckle up, because as "Back to the Future" star Doc Brown (played by Christopher Lloyd) said, "Where we are going, we don't need roads." The chart that follows is a summary of the integrated growth model which represents a road map of our journey together.

Concept 1.1 Grow Now

Concept 1.1 | **8 Essential Steps to Flex Your Leadership Muscles Model**

FLEX YOUR GROWTH LEADERSHIP MUSCLES

8

ADJUSTING YOUR SAILS TO WIN
- "Dirty Dozen" Practical Growth Triangle Concept
- Keeping Score – The Practical Growth Leader Dashboard
- Sailing Around 12 Reefs and Construction Zones
- Rapid Strike Force

7

SPEEDING WITH YOUR STRENGTHS
- Rapidly Emerging Trends/Exponential Rate of Change
- Speeding with Your Strengths Winners
- Speeding with Your Strengths Benefits

6

BUILDING THE GROWTH CURVES
- Building on the Hill Practical Growth Concept
- Where Are You On the Growth Curve?
- Five Growth Stage Questions
- 12 Growth Curve Building Materials
- Simple Squared Growth Concept

5

FINDING THE PASSING ZONES TO FINISH FIRST
- Competitive Attitude
- Fast Passing Zone Concept
- How to Build Your Fast Passing Zone Concept
- Five Rules of the Road
- Running With the 7 Rs

4

FLEXING INNOVATION FLIGHT PLANS
- Finding PAC Power Concept
- Creating the "Fast Break" Innovation Culture
- Chase Gold Growth Segments
- Avoiding Innovation Sand Traps

3

PEDAL TO THE METAL – CUSTOMER LOYALTY NOW!
- Growing Customer Loyalty
- Winning on the Front Lines
- Employer Branding Builds Customer Loyalty
- "Peacetime" Customer Interviews Concept
- Value Creation Relationships

2

REFUELING YOUR GROWTH ENGINES TO WIN THE BATTLE FOR TOP TALENT
- People Leadership
- Why People Leave
- How to keep the Best
- Retention Momentum Bridge Concept
- Coaching With Emotion Every Day Concept
- Hiring the Best People
- Cross-Generational Emotional Connections
- Industry Emotional Connections

1

FLEXING YOUR PRACTICAL GROWTH LEADERSHIP MACHINE
- Find Practical Growth Leaders
- The 8 Cs of The Practical Growth Leader Concept
- Hi/Low Leaders
- G-Factor

"Remember, **fear** is the number one **enemy** of growth."

CHAPTER 1

Step 1: Flexing Your Practical Growth Culture Machine

"Start Me Up!"

It's become an anthem at stadiums across the country as rabid fans eagerly anticipate the opening kickoff. It's also a rock 'n roll anthem that proves Mick Jagger and The Rolling Stones know how to create high passion and energy. Jagger sings, "Start me up! Once you start me up I'll never stop." That is certainly my philosophy when it comes to life because I have a true passion for growing and getting better every day. Find enough leaders with this same passion and you and your teams will be light years ahead of the competition.

Successful Growth cultures are created when an organization or team can create enough critical mass of the right leadership behaviors. We will begin our journey together by differentiating the behaviors that build successful growth leaders and businesses from the ones that can suck the life out of any company or team. There are five leadership personalities in any organization and you can usually spot them immediately on any given day. They are:

1. Practical Growth Leaders
2. Building Inspectors
3. Bad News Employees
4. Turtles Hiding in Their Shells
5. Painful Porcupines

Who Are Practical Growth Leaders?

The first are Practical Growth Leaders. They are the fuel that feeds the growth engine. They are always bringing forward new ideas, new alternatives and innovative ways to think about the business. Practical Growth Leaders are relentless in driving change which will result in superior business results. They have optimistic and realistic goals that are attainable. They know how to give teams clear objectives with measurements, the resources they need to get the job done and the accountability to deliver results. Practical Growth Leaders also create an environment that attracts, supports and encourages the creative innovators in your organization.

Who are the creative innovators? Do you know why Michael Nesmith of The Monkees (the popular made-for-television 1960s rock and roll group) had the time to fiddle around with a guitar and write hit song after hit song? Because his mother Betty Nesmith became tired of ruining page after page of typewriter paper due to typing miscues. She then developed a little product called "Liquid Paper" or "White Out," which allowed the typist to quickly correct mistakes on the page and continue with the project. This product not only revolutionized the business world of the 1960s, it also made her and her family rich beyond their wildest dreams. Those of you who grew up during the computer age may never have used a bottle of "White Out," but believe me, Mrs. Nesmith was a great innovator. She challenged conventional thinking as well as bringing forward new and creative solutions. Speaking of the computer age, You Tube was invented by a trio of innovators named Chad Hurley, Steve Chen and Jawed Karim who had a shared vision of creating a new way to share video content on the internet. The You Tube site shows a wide variety of video content including movie and TV clips, music videos, as well as individual blogging. The domain name "You Tube.com" was activated on February 15, 2005 and previewed to the public shortly after that time, kicking off a revolution of video content sharing across generations. You Tube was named The 2006 Invention of the Year by *Time Magazine* and acquired by Google in November of 2006 for a reported $1.65 billion. My guess is the You Tube team would have enjoyed hanging out with Betty Nesmith. Innovators tend to flock together. Practical Growth Leaders find, hire, encourage and reward the innovators. Practical Growth Leaders highly value innovators because they are always working to find new ways to drive revenue and take costs out of the business. Practical Growth Leaders often create "game changers" that lead to unprecedented growth. The Practical Growth Leaders know that the key to creating transformational change is to cultivate the innovators. The key to your success is to create a culture that attracts and retains Practical Growth Leaders. They, in turn, will find, nurture, love, and recognize the innovators. Practical Growth Leaders who win will recruit, stockpile and retain the most talented innovators in your industry. They will lead you to new ways to grow revenue and take costs, as well as time, out of your business processes.

You will find Practical Growth Leaders at all levels of the organization. They anticipate, simplify, innovate, challenge, encourage, listen, emotionally connect, and respond. They live just within the boundaries and are usually one or two steps away from being out-of-bounds. They are usually one step ahead of the corporate posse that is frustrated by their tendency to push the envelope.

They are always trying to push the organization outside of their comfort zone. They sometimes ask for forgiveness rather than permission. Practical Growth Leaders are usually challenged and forced to defend their actions throughout the organization. The courage to become a Practical Growth Leader lives inside every one of us.

Building Inspectors

The second group to scrutinize is Building Inspectors. They are always finding road construction zones and barriers. They delight in highlighting areas where the Practical Growth Leaders' ideas will not work. They are continually talking about why things cannot move forward. Building Inspectors are designed to resist change and aggressively promote the status quo. Imagine if an Apple employee would have made this statement: "This internet thing sounds too complicated. It will never work." Believe me, that building inspector would be escorted out of his or her office, with a pink slip in one hand, a box of personal items in the other. That is the classic example of a Building Inspector. Find the Building Inspectors and ask them to become the Practical Growth Leader's helpers. Senior executive teams/committees are often great Building Inspectors. They love to kick the tires and give movie critic-like reviews - thumbs up or thumbs down - but usually send the team back for more re-work. The Building Inspectors can be valuable only if they question, encourage, help and support the Practical Growth Leaders. If they do, then the final product can be better. However, if they don't, they will ultimately defeat your team. Ask the Building Inspectors to help the Practical Growth Leaders or ask them to leave your organization. They will need to make a career choice. How many times have each of us told someone why a new idea will not work? Beware; it is a dangerous trap for any of us to fall into easily.

Bad News Employees

Next we have what I call Bad News Employees. They just really enjoy a bad business accident. You will hear these accident chasers say things like, "Can you believe the financials in that proposal? I can't wait to see how this disaster turns out." George Costanza (played by Jason Alexander) on "Seinfeld" once said "If you can't say something bad about a relationship, you shouldn't say anything at all." George would have been a model Bad News Employee. They wait outside your office in the morning and cannot wait to share the latest problems. Bad News Employees rarely bring viable solutions with them to solve the problems they share so readily with others. They are cynical in their view of the team and the organization. They are often very effective in their functional responsibilities and are valued by the organization because of their technical expertise. They actually enjoy seeing others fail. These Bad News Employees burn up a lot of calories pursuing, discovering and delivering information about the misfortune of others. They believe they actually add value by playing this role. Have you ever secretly enjoyed hearing about the misfortunes of a fellow team member?

Hiding Turtles

Next come Turtles Hiding in Their Shells. They stick their head inside their shells at the first sign of trouble. Their goal is to survive until the next round. They only stick their heads out when "the coast is clear." Do you want this type of person standing in the fox hole next to you in the daily battles your company fights to stay ahead of the game? I don't. Many of them are administrators with a long tenure. They believe if they can just survive, that "This too will pass." They are very risk averse and don't want to "rock the boat." They salute every objective and budget cut, and usually deliver a large hammer within the four walls of their own world simply to make their numbers. Have you ever played it safe and waited until the storm clouds pass to come out of your shell? Did you ever stay on the sidelines to protect yourself when you could have jumped in with both feet to help support the team?

Painful Porcupines

Finally we have Painful Porcupines. They make everything harder and more complicated. They are negative and abrasive about almost everything. They invented the "not invented here" syndrome. When you see their name on your calendar for a 10 a.m. meeting, you grimace because you know the day just got a lot more difficult. Painful Porcupines usually survive by projecting well upward while having poor relationships with their peers and direct reports. They are combative, defensive and have trouble working with and leading their teams. Practical Growth Leaders generally try to work around the painful porcupines in order to efficiently get things done. They usually are strong from a technical expertise standpoint. They tend to have very poor collaboration and communication skills when they are in the porcupine mode. Do you know any Painful Porcupines?

Look in the Mirror

This book will show you how to become a Practical Growth Leader. The truth is, parts of these five different types of leadership behaviors live within each of us. Take a good, hard look in the mirror. Depending on the circumstances and situation, we have all been Practical Growth Leaders, Building Inspectors, Bad News Employees, Turtles Hiding in Their Shells and Painful Porcupines. I know if I look at myself objectively in the mirror I have been all five of these behavior types with different people. Think about it, while you are all thinking about the painful porcupines you know, make a mental note of people in your life that you think may put you on that same list. I can tell you that I have behaved like a Practical Growth Leader in a 9 a.m. meeting and turned into someone else's Painful Porcupine by a 10 a.m. session. I usually took on these negative behaviors when I felt personally threatened. The truth is we are all guilty of these bad behaviors. We all must make a commitment to behave like Practical Growth Leaders all the time to create a growth culture. Ask yourself at the end of each day, which of the five categories was I most like today? A Practical Growth Leader wins by stockpiling the best team, and challenging it to play to win. The Building Inspectors who convert this behavior into a helping role can make the Practical Growth Leaders more effective. The goal should be to eliminate any individual characteristics where we mirror Bad News Employees, Turtles in Their Shell and Painful Porcupines. This may not be easy, but it will be worth it!

Behaviors Are Contagious

It is also important to remember that the people you lead will take on your behavior characteristics and follow your example. If you come to work tomorrow behaving like a Practical Growth Leader, your team will tend to mirror this behavior. If you show up as a Painful Porcupine, your team will quickly follow your lead.

You know the old saying, "He or she who has the most toys wins." Well, that's not true when it comes to achieving real and sustainable growth. At the end of the day, the CEO who has the most and best people living their business careers as Practical Growth Leaders is the real winner. If you interview new candidates to join your team that do not demonstrate Practical Growth Leader behaviors in their past career experiences, do not hire them. I am reminded of the U2 song "I Still Haven't Found What I'm Looking For." Keep looking for the right leaders and do not settle for anything less, to help you grow the business. Remember in the end, it is all about creating a critical mass with Practical Growth Leader behaviors to generate enough innovation, passion, energy and focus to fuel a growth culture.

Growth Leadership Behaviors:
Become Practical Growth Leaders

Key Characteristics We All Have In Our DNA

Practical Growth Leaders	- New ideas - Innovation - Challenge boundaries/conventional thinking - Champions of growth initiatives - Brings forward new insights
Building Inspectors	- Puts up barriers and construction zones - Why it won't work - We tried it before... we can win with the same playbook - Keep the status quo
Bad News Employees	- Love to see a bad corporate accident - Very cynical - Undermine all proposals - Enjoy berating co-workers
Turtles Hiding in Their Shells	- Keep your nose clean and do your job - Stay away from controversy - Avoid conflict, don't get involved, and this too will pass - Risk avoidance
Painful Porcupines	- You feel pain when you see their name on your calendar - Everything becomes harder when you work with them, every issue becomes more complicated - Sucks energy out of the organization - Tends to be combative and/or passive/aggressive

Hi/Low Practical Growth Leaders

What is a Hi/Low Practical Growth Leader? There are three types of leaders you will interview for any important job. I find this to be true for organizations of all sizes. The first are leaders who understand how to create very powerful strategic constructs, but can't implement anything. The second are leaders who deliver operational excellence at a very high level, but are unable to develop a future vision or strategy to save their lives. The third type of leader, who is a real gem and difficult to find, is the Hi/Low Practical Growth Leader. This individual can develop powerful strategic models and a clear vision while delivering operational excellence. As Practical Growth Leaders, we must learn to do both very effectively. A clear strategic construct combined with operational excellence and a passion for growth represents the foundational skills you need to become a Practical Growth Leader. One of the key reasons companies of all sizes struggle to achieve their goals is that they are unable to recruit and grow leaders that have these critical skills. Why do you think the San Francisco 49ers won four Super Bowls with Joe Montana at quarterback? Montana was a leader who understood what was needed to motivate his team at the critical time! When the chips were down, and his back was against the wall, Joe Cool was at his best. On the game-winning drive in Super Bowl XXIII, the legendary quarterback could sense his team was in panic mode. In the huddle, before he threw the game-winning touchdown pass to John Taylor, Montana said, "I don't believe it." His teammates looked to him, and he grinned. "John Candy is sitting in the stands over there." They smiled, relaxed and claimed a 26-21 victory. Teams must be managed according to the situation around them. Practical Growth Leaders must be able to fly a 747 at 35,000 feet or a Cessna at a few hundred feet above ground. If they do, they will know what is needed to motivate their team at the critical time. The Hi/Low Practical Growth Leader style creates the future and brings it alive throughout the organization. The truth is most companies, large or small, do not have enough Hi/Low leaders in key roles. This causes strategy and implementation to become disconnected. These connection problems often lead to a steady stream of consultants who develop new strategies, an operational group executing a strategy they don't understand or believe in and a senior management team that lacks focus and continually chases after the latest mousetrap or a new butterfly.

G-Factor

G-Factor means understanding the most minute details of your business. G-Factor is a key component of the Practical Growth Leaders tool chest. By understanding the granular details of your business, you build credibility throughout the organization and gain knowledge that plays a critical role in strategy development. Why has Procter & Gamble historically required its brand managers to work in their sales organizations? Why does Wal-Mart have a passion about its senior executives working in stores all week -- going all the way back to Sam Walton? What are you doing with your team right now to get closer to the business? Bill Belichick is a mild-mannered coach who wears a hoody on the sidelines and says about seven words per post-game news conference. The media in the New England area says he's about as exciting as watching paint dry. Yet his players respond to his low-key approach and would march into hell with him if he asked. That's why his Patriots have won multiple Super Bowls. He also takes a granular, detailed approach into each game. His week-to-week defensive schemes have become legendary. You have to have trust and credibility with your employees, those folks who mean the most to you and your company. As a Practical Growth Leader, you can get more granular details about your business by circulating with the front line troops:

- Working with sales associates every day
- Visiting with your suppliers about how to improve the value chain
- Walking the floors of your production facilities
- Facilitating two-way communication (real time) between front-line employees and senior leaders
- Going on sales calls
- Peacetime Customer Interviews with no selling agenda

These tactics break through the barriers and enable Practical Growth Leader G-Factor. This is not a brand new concept among successful leaders. Abraham Lincoln understood the G-Factor and the value of circulating among his front-line troops to build it. He relieved General John C. Fremont of Missouri in September of 1861 because he refused to interact with his troops and lost touch with the very issues he was trying to resolve. Lincoln knew his best generals worked closely along the front line talking to their troops and using those conversations as input to develop their strategies. Had it not been for the insightful Lincoln to turn the North's reigns over to Ulysses S. Grant, who knows what the final outcome of the Civil War might have been. This is a good story to remember when you are debating whether or not to ride along with one of your people on that next sales call! We must all work hard every day to find the G-Factor and not follow the path of least resistance. It is also good to remember that the No. 1 reason Lincoln chose Grant was he knew how to fight and win.

Add Passion and Energy

Passion and energy are both free. Practical Growth Leaders spread passion and energy throughout every level of your organization. Look in the mirror each morning and make a promise to yourself that you will bring them with you to work everyday. In the 1987 movie "Wall Street," Gordon Gekko (played by Michael Douglas), with his hair slicked back and the veins in his neck bulging, delivered the famous line: "Greed is good." He was referring to the fuel that drives the market and cadence on Wall Street every day. The Practical Growth Leader must embrace the belief that passion is good and make it the priority. Every successful Practical Growth Leader has a huge dose of passion and energy. Think about great business leaders who have made growth a top priority in their lives. Examples of leaders with passion and energy include Sam Walton, Walt Disney, J.C. Hall, Jack Welch and Lee Iacocca. These individuals all had passion, energy, granularity and a clear vision of the future they wanted to create. They also understood that you evolve a clear vision every day by making things happen. As Walt Disney once said, "The way to get started is to quit talking and begin doing."

Emotional Connections Make the Difference

Practical Growth Leaders know that emotion plays a major role in making business decisions. Film critic Roger Ebert said, "Your intellect may be confused, but your emotions will never lie to you." How true! Emotion oftentimes gets a bad rap in business. People usually say something like, "Don't let emotion get in the way of making the right decision." The fact is, the biggest decisions you make in life are emotional. Is the decision you make to get married a rational or an emotional decision? I met my wife Christine, in April of 1983 and got married in August. There was nothing rational about that decision. My parents were scared to death. It worked out very well for me! Is the decision you make to have kids a rational or emotional decision? Did you sit down and do a list of the pros and cons and decide to have kids? I doubt it! These are major life-changing decisions. The decision to join or leave a company is also a life-altering emotional decision. The best talent makes an emotional decision when it leaves your team or company. It will be presented by the employee in a rational way usually involving proof points: they are leaving for "a better job," "more money," "more experience," or to "pursue a new lifestyle." These reasons generally are smoke screens for the brutal facts that usually cause a high potential team member to leave. The fact is most people really leave because of their relationship with their boss. Also, this dirty little secret is often never talked about in business.

It is in the employee's best interest not to "burn a bridge" with his or her boss and it is in their manager's best interest to position the move as a rational, fact-based decision with the rest of the organization. Few – if any – of these dynamics will surface in Human Resources exit interviews when people leave their company. I will often see exit interview recaps that fail to list management as the reason the individual is leaving an organization. The "breaking news" is that people are rarely candid during the exit interview. They have no incentive to be candid. This posturing also relieves the boss of any personal responsibility. Leaders must have ownership and be personally accountable when their best people leave just as they would be if they lost a major client or customer. This accountability is critical. When the best people leave, growth usually goes out the door with them.

8 Cs of The Practical Growth Leader

Practical Growth Leaders attract and retain the best talent by building powerful, emotional connections with their employees. We will now begin the journey describing the 8 Cs of the Practical Growth Leader:

Concept 1.2

1. Caring
2. Candor
3. Confronting Conflict
4. Circle of Trust
5. Collaboration
6. Credit to Others
7. Communication
8. Celebration

1. Caring

Do you know your team members' dreams? Do you know what really matters to them in the next five years? Do you know what their personal and business priorities are now and in the future? The single most important thing you can do as a leader is not just tell, but show your team how much you care about them as people. Caring is best demonstrated in "unexpected" ways.

Are you engaging the total person or just an employee? This is much more than asking someone how was their weekend. It is more than knowing the name of their spouse or kids. It is much more than sending birthday and holiday cards. Do you know their dreams? Sit down and ask your team members one on one what is really important in their lives and what matters to them. You will be amazed what you learn. You have an opportunity to build a powerful emotional connection and engage the total person. This emotional connection is the most powerful retention device you can build with your top talent. Mary Kay Ash, the CEO and founder of Mary Kay Cosmetics once said, "Pretend that every single person you meet has a sign around their neck that says, 'make me feel important'." You will begin to build a relationship with each team member in a new way. The best time to build these relationships is during breakfast, lunch and dinner. I highly recommend the book *Never Eat Alone,* by Keith Ferrazzi which highlights a practical approach to the melding of business and personal relationships. It is a proven fact that breaking bread together is the best way for you to have these discussions and build an emotional connection with employees and business partners. People are more at ease when they eat together. They remove barriers and let down their force fields. If you are eating breakfast, lunch or dinner alone, you are missing an opportunity to build a relationship.

You will build a powerful connection with your best employees by bringing them help/value vs. a transactional relationship. Find out their dreams and demonstrate that you are committed to developing, growing and helping them to achieve their personal vision of success. You will have to commit the necessary time to do this activity. If you do, you will emotionally connect with your team as a leader who really cares about each of them individually and collectively. Your reward will be a dynamic team that will run through walls for you. If you choose not to invest this time with each team member, you will spend it training and coaching new employees.

We must work hard as we flex our Growth Leadership Muscles. We need to be in the moment with our people. As a proof point, Practical Growth Leaders apply technologies but understand the limitations they have in the workplace. They also understand the power of the personal touch. For example, nasty e-mails are caring relationship killers. Think of the times you have received a flaming e-mail. How do you respond? Do you delete it? Do you respond in kind creating a flaming e-mail escalating arms race? This happens when one e-mail triggers another and more people are copied as the battle escalates. How does a Practical Growth Leader deal with this? When I receive a flaming e-mail, I call the person and say that I received their note and will not be responding via e-mail. I want to meet with them face-to-face to resolve the issue. This resolves the issue quickly and quells future e-mail problems. By the way, guess who is the biggest fan of e-mails in the world of business? The answer is a plaintiff's attorney. It is now one of the first and standard things requested in legal proceedings. Some of the most damaging evidence resulting in large legal judgments has come from e-mail. It is amazing what people will say via e-mail that they would never put in a hard copy note. An e-mail when used properly can have a valuable role to play in business as a way to communicate effectively and efficiently. It can also be a relationship killer. A small business client recently told me she had "outlawed e-mail" from office employees to each other because they were sending e-mails instead of talking to each other when their offices were next door. I am in no way demeaning technology. It has provided new capabilities and efficiency in the work place. It now plays a crucial role in how real work gets done with speed every day. That said, it is critical that we avoid the misuse of technology.

Former Beatle John Lennon said, "Life is what happens when you are busy making other plans." The explosion of multi-tasking with today's technology underscores his message. It is important to remember in an era of the cell phone, Blackberry, e-mail, teleconferencing and text messaging that the best way to create an emotional connection with your top talent is face-to-face or with personal notes and phone calls. People are communicating more and connecting less than ever before. For example, a handwritten note or greeting card expressing praise for a job well done sent by you to a team member's home address is a powerful way to emotionally connect. Another way is a phone call from you to the spouse or significant other telling them how much a team member has meant to the company this year and how much you appreciate their hard work. If top performers bring their families in to visit the office or you run into them outside of work, do you take the time to tell the family how much their husband, wife, mother, father, son or daughter means to your team? I have done all of these things and they are very powerful emotional connections that will help you retain your best performers. These interactions all focus only on the employees' contribution to the team and do not cross the professional line. Remember, most people on your team want you to be a great leader, and not another friend. As a Practical Growth Leader, use the personal touch to differentiate your approach from other leaders. Engage your team members' dreams and utilize the personal touch to build a powerful new emotional connection. Are you in the moment with your people every day or captivated by the latest technology embodied in a new cool executive toy?

Caring Centerpiece

Wow, I wish someone would have reminded me about the importance of caring and being in the moment before I attended a 1997 sales meeting in Las Vegas. I was late, and I was swamped that week, so I brought a folder of work with me to digest during several early-morning sessions. As one speaker after another delivered their message, I became more and more focused on my individual paperwork. I clearly was not "in the moment" and caring within the 8 Cs of the Practical Growth Leader.

Most sales meetings typically have several candy dishes on the table and you are welcome to help yourself throughout the day. This meeting actually had a candy-tree centerpiece, with smaller versions of popular candy bars hanging from each limb. This was great! I could munch on my favorite candy bars while catching up on my paperwork. Due to the combination of jet lag and the time change, I ate five or six mini-candy bars off the centerpiece because I was starved. Finally, it was lunch time. The host suddenly announced that each of the centerpieces, which she had made for the meeting, would be given away to a lucky winner at each table. Suddenly, I buried my head in my hands! I had eaten the prize at a sales meeting. My only hope was that the winning ticket was under my chair. No such luck! A woman sitting across from me found the winning ticket taped to the bottom of her chair. She jumped up and cried out, "I won! But Jim Welch ate my centerpiece!" The room erupted with hysterical laughter. Red faced, I raced down the hall to the hotel gift shop and bought more candy bars. I made a futile attempt to attach them to the winning centerpiece. Everyone thought it was the funniest thing they had ever seen. I was embarrassed and felt terrible the rest of the day.

How did I get into this fine mess? I did not practice the 8 Cs with caring. And more importantly, I was not living in the moment. I was no better than a boss in the airport, who paid more attention to his or her blackberry than what their direct report is telling them about their daily agenda. Remember to always show caring by "being in the moment." And whatever you do, always have a snack on hand so you don't eat the centerpiece.

Moments Create Super Magic

Lamar Hunt knew how to live in the moment. The soft-spoken sports icon was the guiding force behind the creation of the American Football League and the Kansas City Chiefs. He was one of our nation's great sportsmen and gentlemen. The Texas millionaire was also somewhat of a marketing whiz. He came up with the name of the biggest single-day sporting event in the world – the "Super Bowl." When his Kansas City Chiefs played the first Super Bowl, it was simply called the "AFL-NFL World Championship Game." Hunt believed in selling a product, and a special moment with his young daughter led to him developing the name of the granddaddy of all NFL events.

Think about it. The game and the event have come to be known as Super Bowl Sunday, which over the years has become an unofficial national holiday in communities all across America. The Super Bowl is one of the most watched U.S. television broadcasts of the year, attracting many companies to spend millions of dollars every year on creative showcase TV commercials. Super Bowl Sunday is the second largest U.S. food consumption day following Thanksgiving. Halftime performances have featured everyone from The Rolling Stones to Paul McCartney and every genre of music across the landscape. It has truly become a national unofficial holiday as well as an event that transcends sports and is embraced by virtually every diverse cultural fabric in America. The Super Bowl is a truly special Sunday.

So, how was the name conceived? Did it come from a Madison Avenue creative advertising agency? Did it come from a strategic consultant think tank? Not even close! It came from Hunt, a great innovator.

There were many ideas of what to call the big game ranging from "The Big One" to the original name which was the "AFL-NFL World Championship Game." Hunt thought of the name "Super Bowl" after seeing his daughter with a toy called a Super Ball. The ball currently resides in the Pro Football Hall of Fame in Canton, Ohio.

The media and the NFL embraced the power of Lamar's simple name and began using it over time. Think about it! The Super Bowl was created because Hunt lived his life in the moment. Because he was interested in his daughter and her new toy, a new unofficial holiday called Super Bowl Sunday was born.

Remember, little moments can create super magic. Always try to "be in the moment."

Perfect the Art of Rejection

The Practical Growth Leader also embraces caring by "Perfecting the Art of Rejection." As former Prime Minister of the United Kingdom Tony Blair said, "The art of leadership is saying no, not yes. It is very easy to say yes." When I was responsible for marketing at Hallmark, there were several opportunities to say no to potential partners. It is important to remember that everyone's ultimate fear is rejection. Most people fear rejection more than death. Think about it. You spot the prettiest girl or best looking guy in the high school cafeteria but never approach them. Then, years later, you meet by accident in line at the grocery store. They ask why you never approached them back in high school and you mentally give yourself a swift kick in the pants. Why? The fear of rejection. Why did you not make that tough sales call? If applicable, why have you played your career choices safely? Most of the time, these decisions are based on the fear of rejection. Therefore, as a leader, perfecting the art of rejection is a critical way to build emotional connections. Why is it important? Because you want to create positive ambassadors for your brand among those you have rejected. For example, when you reject a student on a college campus, you need to handle it with a personal touch. That's because they very well may be the roommate of the high potential candidate you are recruiting to help your company grow.

Peacetime Praise

Peacetime Praise is real and authentic. It is another critical caring skill required to flex your Growth Leadership Muscles. This type of praise occurs after a positive event happens. It is the fuel that motivates, as well as facilitates growth. I speak all over the world about growth leadership and I always ask the same questions about praise and get the same answers. I first ask the leaders in the audience, how many leaders in this room regularly praise your people? Almost three-fourths of the leaders in the room usually raise their hands. Then I ask how many people in the room feel like they are receiving too much praise? No one raises their hand in response to this question. There is not enough peacetime praise in most companies. This is often confused with performance reviews and coaching which play very different roles. Real and authentic praise is unconditional and not connected to a coaching session. However, it is important to note that even successful coaching sessions focus on at least 80 percent positive feedback and usually detail one development area at a time. Mary Kay Ash, the founder of Mary Kay Cosmetics, said, "Sandwich every piece of criticism between two thick layers of praise." Go crazy with praise and see what happens. Most leaders are praising their people much less than they think they are every day. I challenge you to take the risk of heaping too much praise on your people.

Wartime Praise

Now that we have reviewed Peacetime Praise and what it brings to the Practical Growth Leader table, what is Wartime Praise? This praise takes place right after a potential growth leader informs you that he or she is leaving your company. You panic. You plead, "Please do not leave! We love you! You are the best leader we have ever had. Please have dinner at my house tonight! What is it going to take to keep you here and change your mind?" This praise is perceived as too little, too late and rarely has any significant impact on the person that has already decided to leave. The battle to retain the person was lost a long time before the resignation.

Caring is the most important thing you can do to create a powerful emotional leadership connection with your team members. When you ask people to define their dreams, stay in the moment with their presence, perfect the art of rejection, and bring forward peacetime praise, you are leading with your heart and reinforcing the emotional connection that can only be built by a caring Practical Growth Leader.

2. Candor

Denny Crane, played to perfection by Emmy winner William Shatner in "Boston Legal," said, "The first rule of thumb of practicing law is always, always promise the client millions and millions of dollars. It's good business." I believe the better long-term growth strategy is to lead with complete candor. Bill O'Reilly often refers to the "no spin zone." These zones are hard to find in business and are critical to future growth. Playing to win requires facing the reality of the brutal facts.

In the 1975 classic suspense thriller, "Jaws," police Chief Martin Brodie (played by Roy Scheider) is chumming a gooey concoction of chopped up fish into the ocean, in hopes of enticing a great white shark to surface so he and his crew can destroy it. When it rears its head – which is just about the size of a Volkswagen, he mutters, "We need a bigger boat." Brodie was facing reality and he was right. Most senior executive teams won't admit that they "need a bigger boat." In fact, many executives actually create their personal alternative view of realities for personal gain. This behavior is motivated by fear. The number one technique to create an environment where candor rules, is to drive the fear out of your team and organization. Designate a "Jaws Room" where people can go to "battle it out." There is one rule in the "Jaws Room." There will be no repercussions as a result of total and complete candor. You don't need Bill Murray and Dan Aykroyd from the "Ghostbusters" to use their comic charm and ectoplasm to drive away evil spirits, you can do this as a Practical Growth Leader by rewarding candor and open debate as critical qualities that are valued and encouraged. Promote and compensate team members that produce results and utilize candor as a key enabling behavior. Candor is an important ingredient to create and sustain real growth.

Don't let fear take over your management team. You can drive out fear by creating two-way candor devices such as Town Halls and the "In the Pit" sessions, where employees and leaders can "take the gloves off" and have a wide-open discussion about anything. It is truly "no holds barred." We used these methods and achieved great results with several Fortune 500 clients. They were informal interactive meetings between leaders and front-line employees. Remember, fear is a virus that will slow growth as well as inhibit candor and every organization has it. You don't need to be alone in the woods with a hockey-mask-wearing psycho chasing you with a butcher knife to experience fear. Employee interaction (interactive messaging, anonymous feedback devices that challenge leaders, face-to-face meetings) will help drive fear out of your organization. Fear is a growth killer. It will cause your best people to leave your company and leave the best ideas on the cutting room floor.

Candor is one of the most critical characteristics to become a Practical Growth Leader. If you fail to practice total candor, you will lose the trust of your team, your leadership and your customers.

3. Confront Conflict

Practical Growth Leaders must seek, confront and resolve conflicts. It's really that simple. It is critical that you and your team have a clear understanding of their current reality, where the conflict exists and a culture that openly talks about the big elephants on the table. Think about it. Often we do not want to deal with a major issue because of our fear of how it will impact the relationships. William James, an American philosopher, once said, "Whenever you are in conflict with someone, there is one factor that can make the difference between damaging the relationship and deepening it. That factor is attitude." At Hallmark, I introduced challenge flags at one of our marketing town hall meetings with over 250 people. I opened the meeting by indicating that while

I am not a stupid person, I make two to three stupid decisions every week. I told the team to throw their new challenge flags (each employee received one) to openly question any decision made by any leader in the division. This was done to create a culture of identifying and confronting conflict. It created an environment that made it painless and fun to challenge any decision. People also used the flags to laugh and have fun throwing them in meetings. Laughter is a powerful way to deal with conflict. It can reduce tension and drive out fear. Remember the words of Dr. Maya Angelou: "I am serious, so I laugh a lot. You need to laugh. You don't laugh enough. I don't trust anyone who doesn't laugh." Those are powerful words about the role laughter plays in building trust. If you decide to actually do the flags to help create a conflict friendly culture, I would suggest you use a safe, light substance to make sure the challenge flags avoid any potential safety issues when employees throw them at each other! You must create a culture that welcomes conflict like a special guest to a holiday party. Confronting conflict and taking on the big elephant on the table can create breakthrough bridges to growth. If you use a bit of creativity, confronting conflict can become second nature in your culture.

4. Circle of Trust

Robert DeNiro referred to the circle of trust in the movie "Meet the Parents," when he was outlining the rules of his new relationship with future son-in-law Ben Stiller, who played Greg. "If you step outside the 'circle of trust,' Greg, there is no coming back in. Remember the circle of trust." It is critical to you as a Practical Growth Leader that you have the trust of your team. Remember Joe Montana's cool approach in the closing minutes of that Super Bowl victory? His team trusted him and that trust led to a world championship. This means that you can share confidential information with your team and trust that it will never leave the room. I have used terms like the circle of trust, progressing to "the double dome of silence," and the ultimate "plutonium dome of silence." They all mean the same thing to the team. What is said inside these four walls must stay within the team. Years ago, there was a sign in the Kansas City Royals' clubhouse that read: "What you see here, what you say here, let it stay here, when you leave here." It was comical, but it got the message across to players and other visitors. By laughing among the team, you can use fun phrases to take your collective trust to the next level. This is also crucial if you want to build an environment that encourages candor and confronting conflict. The circle of trust will take the team commitment to growing your business to a new place. Conversely, if you avoid sharing important information with your team or use information as power only telling them what you think they "need to know" to do their jobs, you will lose the hearts of your people. They will question and begin to lose trust in you as a leader. The casualty of this outcome will be the unconditional trust needed to drive sustainable growth.

5. Collaboration

The best way to collaborate and play to win is to utilize the CEO rule and hire people who are smarter than you. At Hallmark, I always tried to be "the great collaborator." The foundation of this collaboration skill was based on a 360 degree leadership effectiveness style that treats every employee like the CEO. Think about it. If you treat every team member the same way you treat your CEO, life would get a whole lot better. They will run through walls for you. Your team will begin to work together like a well rehearsed choir. Music legend Paul McCartney, who some might remember from The Beatles while others remember his career with Wings, said, "I love to hear a choir. I love the humanity... to see the faces of real people devoting themselves to a piece of music. I like the teamwork. It makes me feel optimistic about the human race when I see them cooperating like that." What a powerful way to describe the positive impact that effective collaboration can have on creating a growth culture in your company.

Do you know leaders who project up well in the organization, but struggle with their peers and direct reports in their business relationships? This dynamic is often created because the leader treats their boss different from their peers and their own team. This usually happens without the leader even knowing it. I always believed if I treated everyone like the CEO, I would be successful. Treating people in a different manner, based on their level or status in your organization, will suck the life out of collaboration. Another key to flexing your growth leadership muscles is to find and hire people smarter than you. How do you define people as being smarter than you? Simply put, they create or do things you cannot do. This is the real strength of hiring a team with diversity in thought and style. The problem is that it is human nature to gravitate toward people that we relate to and are more like we are as a leader. Building a team that has the same strengths and style that the leader brings to the table is a disaster waiting to happen. You must have the courage to build a team that is smarter than you. Practical Growth Leaders understand this philosophy and are not threatened by it. In fact, they use it to stockpile the best innovators on their teams.

In 1972, the O'Jays recorded a song called "Love Train." I often use the term, "Get on the love train" to reinforce that we will debate vigorously and support uniformly. You want to invite confronting conflict and make sure all the pros and cons are put on the table. However, once the decision is made, the team must support it and each other when you all leave the room. Have fun with your team by invoking the O'Jays hit song and say it's time to, "Get on the Love Train." One of the biggest obstacles to creating a growth culture is that most companies have trouble making a final decision and sticking with it. As "Who Wants to be a Millionaire?" host Regis Philbin would ask, "Is that your final answer?" Too often, the answer in most companies is "No." Practical Growth Leaders must build a culture that makes the dreaded second meeting an unacceptable option. The second meeting is a discussion that happens after the final decision is made that only includes select members of the team who continue to debate and disagree with the decision. Then, the decision is changed again. You will often hear other employees, who feel as if they are left out in the cold by the second meeting, say, "When is a decision a decision?"

An effective Practical Growth Leader is no different than an NFL quarterback who breaks huddle and heads to the line of scrimmage to call the play. The time for debate is in the huddle. Once the team is moving forward to execute the play, the time for debate is over. You can't debate the play once the signal is called.

When Len Dawson was quarterbacking the Kansas City Chiefs, he was called the "Quiet Assassin." One of his teammates once said, "Len just had this look. It was more painful than a kick in the chops. If you got that look from Len, you just wanted to go crawl under a rock. We all respected him and whatever Len said in the huddle was it. No one questioned him because he knew what he was doing out there." This happens in most organizations every day. As a Practical Growth Leader, promote vigorous debate and make sure the team locks arms and moves forward together once a decision is made. Team trust in decisions will build team confidence and help defeat fear, which is the mortal enemy of growth.

"Watch Out For the Roof"
COLLABORATE!

If you work hard to collaborate, you will make better decisions. If you isolate yourself from others, you will "leap before you look" – and the end result could be either embarrassing or frustrating, or a bit of both.

In 1986, I was traveling in New York and stayed at a small, quaint hotel. After checking in late one night after a television commercial shoot, I took the elevator with a work associate. We went up to the third floor and he got off and said good night. I was now in the elevator by myself. As the elevator continued to ascend, suddenly, it stopped between floors with a loud thud. There I was all alone in my hotel's elevator at 11:00 p.m. My mind wandered back to all the situation comedies I had viewed, ranging from Laura Petrie giving birth to Ritchie on an elevator in the "Dick Van Dyke Show," to Jerry and George trying to spot a young woman Jerry had flirted with the night before at a party as she exited an elevator in her business office on "Seinfeld."

However, I must admit that this was no laughing matter. Suddenly, a voice comes over the elevator speaker from the lobby. "We know you are in there. The engineer is on his way to fix the elevator. He lives in New Jersey. He won't be here for another 30 to 45 minutes." That amount of time feels like an eternity when you are stuck in an elevator.

The elevator started to make a loud noise and slip down a couple of notches without warning. I won't say that my life flashed before my eyes, but I do remember seeing something about an early childhood birthday party and a trip to the zoo. Suddenly, there was another thud and the elevator began to ascend very quickly going faster and faster. I grabbed my briefcase and overnight bag and made the decision that if this elevator ever stops and the door opens, I am leaping out.

The elevator stops, and I leap out, taking everything with me. I look up. I see stars! I am now on the narrow roof of this quaint Hotel. I tried to leap back on the elevator and the door closed. I ran to the stairway door and it is locked. I am now stranded on the roof of the hotel. It was August and the temperature that day was close to 100 degrees. If I'd had a couple of eggs in my briefcase, I could have fried them on the shingles. The air conditioners are roaring and it is dark and desolate on top of a tall, skinny building. It was 1986 and there was no access to cell phones, Blackberries, or wireless connections of any kind!

Meanwhile, the engineer arrives from New Jersey, fixes the elevator and brings it floor by floor back to the lobby. The door opens up and the engineer calmly asks, "Where is the guy that you said was stuck in the elevator?" They conducted a floor by floor search and finally found me on the roof. The hotel staff was wonderful and gave me a great room for the evening, which I appreciated. Little did I know that one day, that wild adventure would be a part of a book.

The moral is simple: I was isolated, alone - with a sense of urgency to do something fast and I made a mistake. If someone had been with me, they might have said, "Hey Jim, don't jump... there are stars out there... we are on the roof!" I had no one to collaborate with to consider the potential implications of my action. Surround yourself with people smarter than you. Listen, ask questions, and carefully consider the implications. Whatever you do, collaborate so you can "stay off of the roof." It is a lonely place when you decide to go it alone. Gen. Norman Schwarzkopf, the United States Army Commander during the Gulf War, said, "There's more than one way to look at a problem, and they all may be right." I would have been much better off if I would have had Stormin' Norman on that elevator with me.

6. Credit to Others

President Harry Truman once said, "It is amazing what can be accomplished when no one cares who gets the credit." That is a great growth leadership philosophy. It is critical that the Practical Growth Leader gives all the credit to other team members. This will help to create a high energy environment where new innovators emerge. You must publicly and tangibly reward the innovators. Remember, it is not all about you. When George Brett led the Kansas City Royals to the 1985 World Series championship, his teammate Mark Gubicza said, "We just climbed on George's back and he took us to the title." Yet Brett said, "We did this together, as a team." Don't you know his teammates loved him when he made that comment?

Public praise and recognition in front of the entire team is a powerful technique to create a highly motivated growth culture. When I was with Hallmark we created something special called the Marketing Excellence Awards. The nominations primarily came from peers and were recognized every month in our marketing town hall meetings. We had 12 grand-prize winners at the end of the year featuring a cash bonus and engraved mantle clock. Everyone who was nominated received flowers and small gifts from the team. Since these nominations came primarily from the team, it was a great way to celebrate their accomplishments in front of everyone. People were genuinely moved when they walked up to receive them in front of the entire team. I saw many Marketing Excellence Award winners, including managers and administrative assistants, with tears in their eyes when their names were called. While the bonus dollars were relatively small, the recognition in front of the entire peer group across the generations made it a day to remember. If you can create a memory that will last a lifetime, you will have an employee who would never think about taking another job.

Credit to others is a great leadership trait when the team wins. However, when the team loses, the Practical Growth Leader always takes full accountability and "goes down with the ship." Don Shula, the only NFL coach to ever enjoy an undefeated season, said, "When we win, I get too much credit. When we lose, I get too much blame. But it doesn't matter to me; that's just life." Team members must be protected so that we can live to fight another day and continue to take risks. I used to tell my team that it was my job to take the sniper's bullet and step in front of any team member in harm's way to assume full responsibility and accountability.

As Simon and Garfunkel crooned, "Like a bridge over troubled waters, I will lay me down." Now, I can't carry a tune in a bucket, but if you consistently do this, your team will respond in a fashion that is both positive for you, them and your organization. If you do not, your best people will lose trust in you as a leader and leave your team inhibiting your future growth capabilities. It is also critical that you encourage the team members that did outstanding work to personally present to top management so their work can be recognized. This allows you to give credit to others while building a strong circle of trust throughout your team. If you constantly give credit to others, you actually receive more credit from your team and management for being a great leader. If you take the sniper's bullet and go down with the ship during troubled times, you will receive a great deal of credit for how you responded to the problem. It will not be a fun position to take during the tough times. However, as country music icon Dolly Parton once warbled, "If you want the rainbow, you've got to put up with the rain."

Look for creative and fun ways to give credit to others. I had a passion about achieving retail sales increases. I challenged my Hallmark team to achieve a retail sales increase for 1994 Mother's Day when I was the general manager responsible for seasons. I promised the team that I would present the results wearing a blue dress. This opportunity was a huge motivator for the team to exceed our retail objective. The team achieved the required increase and I wore the dress complete with a jewelry ensemble in front of the entire season business unit. At 6-foot-2, 220 pounds all dressed up with a blond wig, I looked more like a professional wrestler than anything else. Everyone who was aware of our celebration had a great time on that memorable day. Everyone at Hallmark had a great laugh that day, at my expense. I enjoyed the moment more than any of them. Believe me, it wasn't a drag. I gave the team all the credit. Never underestimate the power of self-effacing humor at the leader's expense to add fun to any team celebration!

7. Communication

Communication is usually the biggest single issue I experience in working with all companies of every size imaginable. Confucius said, "Tell me and I'll forget. Show me and I'll remember. Involve me and I'll understand." This philosophy represents the road map to effective communication. Most companies fail to follow the critical five elements of successful communication.

Win with simple words and be brief. Avoid acronyms and complicated explanations. Think of the more famous speeches ever delivered by our country's great leaders. What did Martin Luther King, John Kennedy, Winston Churchill and Ronald Reagan have in common? They spoke with simple, powerful brevity. Remember the Martin Luther King phrase, "I have a dream." How about when John Kennedy said, "I believe that this nation should commit itself to achieving the goal before this decade is out, of landing a man on the moon and returning him safely to earth." There were the powerful words of Winston Churchill, who said, "Never, never, never give up." Ronald Reagan stared Soviet Union leader Mikhail Gorbachev in the eye and said, "Tear down this wall." These leaders clearly understood that simple words cause emotional connections to stir. These leaders sent powerful messages about the civil rights movement, the importance of the space race and the end of the Cold War. Leaders in business too often get mired in the details of the problem or solution in their communication and lose their teams in the process. How many times have you sat in a meeting only to see the communicating become more and more complex and confusing?

Win by emphasizing two-way communication. This is essential to achieve victory. When most leaders talk about communication with their teams, they talk about the mechanics of the communication (newsletters, intranets, etc.). However, most leaders pay less attention to how two-way communication really occurs in an organization. It is really this simple. If you have a strong two-way face-to-face communication plan, everyone becomes an engaged stakeholder and fear in the organization subsides. If you don't, fear increases as trust erodes, and you no longer have a culture supporting growth. The bad news is the Practical Growth Leaders will ultimately leave your organization. The additional risk is that the Bad News Employees, Turtles Hiding in Their Shell and Painful Porcupines' behavior which lives deep down inside all of us will rise to the surface. When will we decide to switch into a survival mode and ride out the storm?

Tell one story. The most important communication tool is consistency. The fact is everyone on your team usually talks about your message. If your messages are inconsistent, they will quickly lose trust in you as a leader. This flaw always leads to failure. There is a tendency at times to spin the story in different ways depending on the audience. This is a recipe for total disaster, especially when dealing with someone who had just attained the status of a leader. I was often teased by colleagues who said my communication style was from the "Department of Redundancy." Believe it or not, I always viewed that as a positive because an important message takes a great deal more than one communication event. However, I will confess that I was often too repetitive on the same voice mail message.

Respond to feedback with action. It is critical that a Practical Growth Leader responds to employee two-way feedback and places the input into three categories. Yes, we will implement your recommendation utilizing this timeline. No, we will not move forward with your recommendation and here is why. Finally, we need more information to decide whether or not to move forward. Failure to respond with one of these three answers will put you in a deeper hole with your team than if you had not asked for their input in the first place.

Provide a real-time response. It is critical that you respond to two-way feedback quickly. Leaders often make the critical mistake of waiting until they have all the information before responding to employee input. The team is usually taking your growth leadership evaluation down one full letter grade for every week you let go by without responding. It is much better to respond in 48 hours with 80 percent of the information than to wait 30 days until you are 99 percent sure of all the facts and implications.

Remember, when it comes to communication, the goal is to drive fear out of your organization. Fear kills growth. You need to make sure that the in-the-pit communication sessions you have with your employees are peacetime meetings without any other agenda than communication. Peacetime meetings will help drive fear out of your team and help create a growth culture throughout the organization.

8. Celebration

Nothing drives change momentum faster than celebrating your successes along the way. Tom Peters, the author of "In Search of Excellence," along with many other classic books once said, "Celebrate what you want to see more of." Jack Welch, former CEO of General Electric said, "Companies don't celebrate enough when people win. It's all about praising others and getting excited about their victories." I would add that it is also critical to celebrate to build momentum for change. You celebrate by storytelling and reinforcing key actions, accomplishments and behaviors you want to spread as part of changing your culture. Celebration meetings enable the Practical Growth Leader to bring along all the levels of your organization together during periods of transformational change. Organizations too often only bring the senior leaders along for the ride and leave the rest of the organization behind. The momentum that celebration meetings create fuels the passion and energy needed to drive change.

Summary

We have completed Step 1 of the journey where we defined the critical characteristics and behaviors of a Practical Growth Leader. The five leadership behaviors that can be found quickly in any organization underscore the need to become a Practical Growth Leader 365 days a year. This is because the leadership behavior you choose is the one your people showcase every day. The 8 Cs of The Practical Growth Leader build powerful emotional connections with your people and create a powerful foundation for a winning culture. The bottom line is that a successful growth culture is based on leadership that can create emotional connections with their employees every day. It is important to remember that the No. 1 enemy of growth is fear. You need to find the Hi/Low Practical Growth Leaders with the G-Factor to drive business growth. You must also recruit and retain the best innovators by utilizing the 8 Cs of the Practical Growth Leader. The biggest decisions in life are emotional. That includes the decision to come to work every day with your brain and your heart!

What's Next?

We have set the table to create a powerful growth culture through building emotional connections at all levels of your team and organization. It is now time to move on to Step 2 to win the battle for the very best people. The stakes could not be higher. If you fail to win the battle to recruit and retain the top talent, sustained growth will not happen for your business. We will show you the roadmap of how to stockpile and keep the very best people who will ultimately decide your future.

I don't believe in luck, but I do believe in destiny. Remember, as Oprah Winfrey said, "I feel that luck is preparation meeting opportunity." Are you ready to clear the Step 1 hurdle questions and build your 90-day leadership Flex Plan for Growth?

Step 1 Hurdle Test

Are you ready to move to Step 2?

Answer these questions:

1. Who are the Hi/Low Leaders?
2. What is the G-Factor? Why is it critical?
3. What are the 8 Cs of Practical Growth Leadership to emotionally connect with your team?
4. What is the one thing you will do differently to emotionally connect with your team?
5. Why is it important to celebrate your team victories?

90-Day Leadership Culture Flex Plan for Growth

Time Frame	Activity
30 Days	Share the five distinct leadership behaviors in team building session highlighting the need to be Practical Growth Leaders every day. (e.g. vs. Building Inspectors, Bad News Employees, etc.)
	Set up breakfast, lunch, or dinner with your top five performers and ask them "What are your dreams?" Learn what motivates the total person, not just the associate.
60 Days	Share the need to be "in the moment" with your leadership team by avoiding the "misuse of technology multi-tasking trap" (e.g. emails, Blackberry, etc.). Create a culture of calling each other out when you are multi-tasking and not listening to each other. Develop guidelines in writing for the language to be used when saying no to recruits, employees, and customers. If handled correctly, they will become positive Brand Ambassadors.
	Develop fun activities and rituals with your team to promote two-way communication and confronting conflict. Create a special "Jaws Room" to address difficult issues together and

introduce challenge flags (or other fun activities) for each employee to use when they disagree with you or each other.

90 Days   Develop an ongoing communication meeting forum that meets at least once every three weeks only to communicate (two-way) with employees. (No other agenda allowed)

Send personal notes or greeting cards to the spouse or other key influencers of your top three team members acknowledging a specific contribution they have made to the team within the last 60 days and reinforce how much they mean to the team.

Celebrate three team growth success stories.

Step 2: Refueling Your Growth Engines to Win the Battle for Top Talent

The Stakes

Dr. Maya Angelou, the American poet, said, "Talent is like electricity, we don't understand electricity, we use it." In any game, the team with the most talent usually wins. Great coaching and leadership can pull upsets every now and then, confounding the experts and critics. However, in the long run, the team with the most talent usually prevails. This is also true when you cast a motion picture (if you have a good script, great actors and a quality director), create a musical group (The Beatles, The Four Tops, U2, The Eagles), build an airport, or go on a space mission (the earth-bound team that supported the first walk on the moon). At the end of the day, it is all about talent. While this is widely recognized throughout business leadership circles, it is an area that usually receives only lip service from the top leadership of many companies. Too many in top management across companies of all sizes believe great leaders have interchangeable parts that can be easily replaced. Two of the top enemies of the Practical Growth Leader are ignorance and arrogance.

We will highlight the key leverage points you can utilize as a Practical Growth Leader to recruit and retain the very best people. If you follow this roadmap, you will stockpile the best people, which is how you win the game with both customers and your competition. Several key paradigms must be broken and we must be willing to migrate to a new place.

People Leadership

"I don't know the answer. You should call HR to find out." If I had a dollar for every time I heard this phrase over the past 30 years, I would be a wealthy person. Human Resources fulfills an implementation role in most organizations today. Even the term "HR" brings a lot of business baggage to the table. The changing role of Human Resources among Practical Growth Leaders is evolving into a strategic role called People Leadership. What does People Leadership look like going forward?

The emerging and changing role of People Leadership (Human Resources) is dramatic, and can be characterized as evolving from transactional to emotional, from saying no to creative solutions, from divisional (national) to global, from tactical to strategic, and from interchangeable parts to top performers.

Transactional to Emotional

The People Leadership function and role must emotionally connect with the top performers in your organization. The role of Human Resources today is often mired in answering the latest employee relations, legal and benefits questions. The true measure of an effective people leadership function is that they create an emotional connection with high potential associates and leaders within the company. These emotional connections have value with current employees as a retention device because they identify early friction points that can be addressed quickly before they lead to an unhappy high potential person leaving the company unexpectedly.

From Saying No to Creative Solutions

The Human Resources function is mechanically wired to say no. Think about it. It is a classic function that is entrenched in policies, rules and legal liability. That said, the current Human Resources functions do play a vital role in enforcing the legal aspects of the people business. However, outside of the legal and consistency arena, too often the answer to your best employees is this: "Our policy is: We will not allow you to do that." These responses help kill the relationship between the high potential employee and the company. The People Leadership role of the future should involve creative problem solving focused on individual employee needs while, at the same time, maintaining the consistent, ethical and legal standards required by the organization. This will be a difficult needle to thread.

Divisional (or National) to Global

How do you leverage and develop your talent worldwide? If applicable, do you have a global leadership development plan in place that puts the greater good of what is right for the person and the total company above the interests of individual divisions and locations? Sadly, the answer to that question is no for most organizations. The lack of a plan is one of the biggest causes of top executive turnover in global organizations. Regardless of where your borders start or stop, nothing should be placed above the interests of the organization as a whole. A global career succession planning process, that charts a clear path toward growing the future talent base of your best leaders by giving them one challenging assignment after another, is critical to growing your business.

Tactical to Strategic Alignment

People Leadership in the future needs to represent a powerful, independent role reporting directly to the CEO about the development of the current leadership as well as the need to acquire additional talent outside the organization. People Leadership should be as independent as the finance function so it can be ruthlessly objective about the true performance of the talent in the organization. Today, Human Resources too often gets caught up in the grinding politics of the organization because line leaders have their favorites as well as those leaders they don't like to have on their team. Too often, these preferences can be based on relationships and comfort level they have with certain individuals. This is one of the reasons there is often a great deal of turnover when top executives leave an organization. If People Leadership reports in at the top of the organization, it is much easier to resolve major people issues across divisions and locations. Human Resources must play the objective reference in these controversies involving how to best leverage your best people. Outstanding CEOs should spend a very high percentage of their time resolving and making decisions on people issues. The CEO often needs to be directly involved to make the tough people decisions. As Leland McKensie (played by Richard Dysart) of "L.A. Law" fame said, "It's time for you people to remember whose name is at the top of the letterhead." Sometimes, there is no other way to deploy the right talent at the right place at the right time.

Interchangeable Parts to Top Performers are Gold (Keep Them!)

Are you a leader who believes when your top performers leave they can be easily replaced? Do you believe top leadership parts are interchangeable? Or, do you treat the loss of a top performer just like the loss of a major customer? If you do not, you should treat it the same way. Once enough top performers leave an organization, they usually take the sustainable profit dollars right along with them. The reality is that while most companies talk about the importance of retaining their very best people, they do not have specific retention plans in place.

Human Resources Measurements

Human Resources professionals want to measure every training activity. They want to know the impact of every seminar. However, most of these measurements revolve around efficiency. For example, 80 percent of the employees have taken a team building seminar, but only 26 percent have taken more than one. The truth is most of these measurements are worthless. Seek only measures that create value and return for shareholders and customers. For example, 86 percent of the people who took this training had a 35 percent increase in engagement scores and were 50 percent more likely to achieve their revenue and profit objectives for the year. Now, that is something to grab hold of and drive throughout the organization creating value along the way.

Tom Peters, the author of "In Search of Excellence," said, "People are enthusiastic, motivated and totally committed, except the eight hours a day they work for you!" This also applies to training seminars offered by most companies. There has even been a Super Bowl commercial brought to us by CareerBuilder.com which shows stressed out employees running through the jungle desperately wanting to escape from having to volunteer for another training seminar. "It's another all day session!" That is the quote just as they are running through the jungle together to escape more training! There is a natural aversion to these events by your associates. That is why it is critical to tie the training and seminars directly to measures that involve value creation for employees and customers.

Distrust to Trust

Ralph Waldo Emerson, American author and poet, said, "Our distrust is very expensive." The fact is most employees have a "trust issue" with Human Resources and only want to share what they need to know or have to in order to get what they want. The emerging role of People Leadership demands that a bridge of trust be built as part of the emotional connection to employees. The Gallup Organization believes: "The bottom line is, the only organizations that will survive in the long-term are those that truly value their people and customers...those that focus on established long-term relationships with them... based on trust." I truly believe this with all of my heart. Trust in any organization must begin with the People Leadership function. It must also begin with the line leader who is the individual's boss.

Why People Leave

Why do people leave teams and organizations? Remember, the No. 1 reason people leave jobs is because they fail to connect with their bosses as leaders and as people. People are rarely honest about why they leave a company. Too many associates that depart follow Jimmy Conway's advice (played by Robert DeNiro) in the 1990 hit movie "Goodfellas," who told Henry Hill (played by Ray Liotta), "Never rat on your friends and keep your mouth shut." As stated earlier, there is no upside incentive for the employee to be open and honest. Think about it! The primary reason people leave companies is because of the relationship and lack of emotional connection with their boss. However, it is almost never talked about in the exit interview. Why? Who wants to burn a bridge with a boss they may need for a future job reference? It is easier to talk about work/life balance, moving on to build your skill sets, or the need to make more money. Salary is much further down the list as a reason to leave than what is usually reported in exit interviews. What is your current game plan to keep your best people? While most companies talk a great deal about the need to retain the best people to sustain growth, they lack an integrated game plan to create retention momentum. We will now launch into an integrated approach called the Retention Momentum Bridge Concept.

How to Keep the Best

As a leader, you are personally accountable to acquire and retain the very best people to win the game. It is that simple. If you fail to recruit and retain the top talent, you will not sustain growth over time. At the end of the day, the Practical Growth Leader must embrace a plan to retain the very best talent. In the 1970s, Led Zeppelin recorded a classic song called "Stairway to Heaven." The steps highlighted in the Retention Momentum Bridge concept provide a stairway to winning with your best people every single day.

Concept 2.1

Retention Momentum Bridge Concept

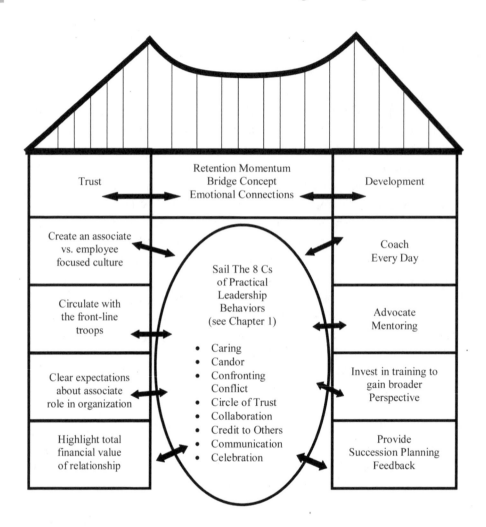

Emotional connections provide the fuel that builds the Retention Momentum Bridge. It is driven by the trust and development of your individual team members. The building blocks under trust and development provide the bridge support. The 8 Cs of The Practical Growth Leader drive energy into each of the supporting bridge blocks accelerating development and building trust. It starts with building your emotional connections with each of your team members.

Emotional Connection Points

The power of the "unexpected" is the most powerful way to emotionally connect with another person. Think about it! Do you get more credit with your significant other when you send a hand written note when they least expect it? Of course you do! The same concept applies to you as a leader. It is the "unexpected" things a leader does that really make the difference. Key examples of "unexpected" leadership behavior include the following:

1. Write a personal handwritten note or send a greeting card to the spouses, mothers or fathers of your best employees telling them what a difference their partner is making to your business.

2. Take the employee to breakfast, lunch or dinner (if appropriate) and ask them what "really matters" to them and what you can do as a leader to help them build their future dreams. "What can I do to better support you?" This is a powerful phrase that shows caring and your vulnerability as a leader.

3. Take your entire team out together to celebrate a special event. For example, when I was with Hallmark, I would take my direct reports out every year for a holiday dinner in the private dining room of a local restaurant. I would go around the room and say something special about each of the team members at the end of the meeting. These comments would focus more on the unique strengths of the individual team members rather than any specific accomplishments they achieved during the year. The primary message delivered in front of the entire team focused on the unique skill sets each person brings to the table throughout the year to make us all successful.

4. Place a call to a significant influence or key family member in their lives. You should make phone calls to fathers and mothers if you believe it will make a difference to your best employees. Always ask permission first if you are going to contact anyone beyond the spouse. It is impossible to know without asking whether a call to someone's parents would be comfortable for an employee or not. You also should follow any laws or rules regarding employee privacy.

5. Create a surprise, fun outing as part of a team business trip. I took my

team on a business trip together to the West Coast. While on the trip, we made an "unexpected" stop at "The Rock," or Alcatraz in San Francisco. We took the night tour which has an entirely different flavor from the daytime excursions. You have not really bonded as a team until you have stood together next to Al Capone's cell at night on the island of Alcatraz. It provides a whole different perspective on your team's day-to-day challenges and opportunities. It puts all of your team and individual challenges in perspective. These are team bonding experiences that people remember.

6. Create local, fun activities for the team that range from taking them on hiking trips and picnics to bowling under disco lights and attending shows/live plays. These events are fun team activities that should be done during regular business hours to truly be appreciated. Weekend team activities that cut into individual personal time are almost always guaranteed to land with a giant thud. Remember, your team wants you to be a great leader. They are not looking for another weekend friend.

7. Utilize your boss to deliver special praise for a job well done in a one-on-one meeting with your team member. If you are not a CEO, you can engage the person you report to, to conduct a one-on-one meeting with your best performing team members. Again, this meeting should be unexpected and focus on results and accomplishments as well as the recognition of the unique strengths of the individual. If you are a CEO, having a key member of the Board of Directors call one of your best people just to tell them how much they are appreciated will go a long way toward retention.

8. Create an unexpected personalized memento for individual team members celebrating the accomplishment of a major event—for example, fun team picture albums personalizing each individual's role and special memories the team experiences together.

Retailer Connection

The Ace and TrueValue Hardware retailers are increasingly utilizing the 8 Cs of The Practical Growth Leader with their employees to focus on improved associate and customer engagement. Ron Cox, an Ace Hardware owner in Appleton, Wisconsin, represents a great example of emotionally connecting with his employees. Ron sent a handwritten note and gift card to the significant other of each of his star employees to let them know how much their spouse meant to his store as a highly valued employee and person. Ron's staff members were honored and their spouses were thrilled. Ron plans to continue this approach with a number of his key employees in the future. Ron is a proactive, engaged Practical Growth Leader. These emotional connections will be transferred to the customer as Ron's staff "pays it forward." In the 2000 movie "Pay It Forward," Kevin Spacey indicated that sometimes the smallest things make the biggest difference and by using random acts of kindness you can "pay it forward." This will work very well from you to your employees and in turn to your customers.

Big Foot

I have always had a habit as a leader of stomping my feet when I walk down the hallway. People could always hear my size 12 loafers before we made visual contact. This habit has followed me throughout my career. By the way, I also had trouble keeping my shirt tail tucked in at all times. During my early years I was counseled to walk slower and talk lower if I really wanted to move into senior management ranks. My teams always had fun with my foot stomping on a regular basis. In fact, I was given the unexpected gift of a "big boot" from my team that was placed on a plaque with the inscription "Big Foot... Keep on Stompin." Everyone had a great deal of fun with this award at my expense. I loved it!

Combine all of these emotional connections with self-effacing humor. Always remember, humor at the expense of your team almost always removes deposits from the emotional connection bank. Take your job seriously, but go crazy making fun of yourself. Your team will love it. Humor also relaxes your team and reduces tension. I am a very focused and intense leader and humor helps lighten a stressful situation. Why was the movie and television series "M*A*S*H" so successful? They conveyed humor that was so necessary to maintain sanity in the blood-drenched horror of the front lines during the Korean War.

The 50-Yard Line

Some of my best memories have always been when the team responded back in a caring and unexpected way to me as a leader. It makes you feel like you have really connected with them. I want to share some personal stories about those special moments.

I turned 50 in 2004, which is a unique time in most everyone's life. You begin to realize you have less in front of you than you do behind on the road you have traveled. In August of 2004, my team surprised and delighted me as a leader. I am a huge fan of the Kansas City Chiefs. I am a season ticket holder who attends almost every home game. This becomes important as the story unfolds. The team came to my office and blindfolded me. They drove me around blindfolded in the car for some time. I felt like a cast member in the movie "Goodfellas" or "The Godfather." I was walked onto some grass and it felt like we were outside at a park. Then, they told me to look down as they took off the blindfold. There I was looking at the 50-yard line at Arrowhead Stadium. We took a tour of the facilities and had a barbeque lunch in the press box. My family was also in on it and attended the party. Finally, they even had my boss and the CEO call me at the stadium, putting me on, wondering why I was missing a critical meeting and demanding an explanation. A great time was had by all. More importantly, I had never been more proud of the relationship I had with my team than I was that day. A picture of me at the 50-yard line will always be on display in our home. It was the proudest day of my career. It was much more important to me than any business award or accomplishment.

Home Turf

Don't forget how the little things can make a huge difference. For example, instead of always having your people meet with you in your office, go visit them on their home turf. It is a sign of mutual respect. The ironic part is that by going to their home base, you give up your legitimate management authority to that person. They will actually see you as a more powerful, confident and caring leader. The location of the meeting is a little thing that makes a big difference. You will increase your effectiveness as a Practical Growth Leader when you visit your people's home turf regularly. It is a sign of reverence and respect, showing that you care as much for them as individuals as you do for them as professionals.

Make Time to Connect

Remember, people do not usually leave organizations. They leave their leaders. If you lose enough good people, your organization will be unable to grow. The Practical Growth Leader understands that emotional connections to the leader are the most powerful retention devices in the tool kit.

If this is all true, why do leaders so often fail to build these emotional connections with their people? Because it takes time and places many leaders outside their comfort zones, thus increasing their vulnerability. It is easier to tackle those 85 e-mails sitting in your in-box. What many leaders fail to realize is that they are actually more vulnerable if they choose not to invest the time to do it. How does the time needed to replace all your top talent compare with the investment you need to make to emotionally connect with your people? You need to invest every day.

Coach Every Day

Most performance reviews and appraisals are a total waste of time. Many companies use them as documentation to protect themselves if they ever have to fire or discipline a given person. They actually protect the employee because many leaders lack candor. Have you ever tried to fire a poor performer only to discover their last three reviews have been stellar? It happens all the time in corporate America. There are legitimate reasons that the performance review process must exist. However, true individual growth only occurs when a leader commits to coaching every day. What do I mean by coaching every day? A Practical Growth Leader commits to coaching the individual during or immediately after the event occurs. Coaching is about the good, bad and ugly. If you coach your people when the event occurs, they will be much more open to coaching on the issue than they will be seven days (or even 24 hours) later.

The absolute prime directive of coaching is to never surprise your employees at their mid-year or annual review with something you have not shared with them before. Have you ever heard a leader say, "I will handle that issue with them at their mid-year review." This is a big mistake. It creates an environment of distrust around the performance review process. People should never go into their formal reviews waiting for a surprise or for the other shoe to drop.

Coaching Everyday Techniques

A critical aspect of being an effective Practical Growth Leader is coaching every day. After an event happens, pull that employee aside privately and first ask about what just happened. What did they experience and how can they get better? Once they have answered these questions, you need to provide coaching feedback. Here are five key techniques you should use to provide feedback.

1. Always start with the positives. What (if anything) did the associate do

right that they should feel good about for the future?

2. Don't "couch" the negatives. Tell it like it is in straight-forward simple language. People hate corporate business speak. Just tell them what they need to do to get better. Try to coach only one development area at a time.

3. Jointly identify future events where the associate can leverage their new learning (based on your feedback) and put it into action. Make the coaching future-oriented.

4. Reinforce the positive aspects so the associate can leverage even more in future business events.

5. End with an emotional connection based on your relationship with the associate. (smile, handshake, acknowledgement of future, activity together, etc.) Always ask them how they feel about your coaching advice.

Concept 2.2

Practical Coaching with Emotion Every Day Concept

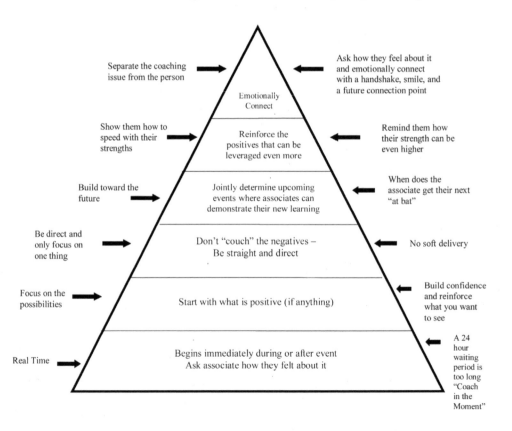

Coaching Blunders

Most leaders make common mistakes when it comes to coaching. The common pitfalls of coaching are highlighted below.

1. Coach your people in real time. Delayed feedback usually results in a negative outcome. A delay of even a few hours is too long and creates associate defense mechanisms against coaching. Also, the time element expanded actually makes it feel to the employee that this is a very important issue regarding their future employment. This may result in very mixed signals being sent by the leader to the associate. When you are coaching, you are working against the clock. It is important to move fast.

2. There is also a temptation for many leaders to immediately jump to the coaching issue. They don't even bother to acknowledge the key things the associate did right. This style can feel more like a professional and even personal attack by the leader against the team member rather than coaching. Don't ever forget the power a leader derives from being positive first!

3. Many times leaders want to soften the blow by carefully "couching" the feedback so they can protect their relationship with the employee and avoid any overreaction to the negative message. This often results in more mixed signals, confusion and frustration on the part of the employee. Conflict avoidance destroys trust and ruins relationships over time. Try to focus your message only on the behaviors the employee can control, and be direct.

4. There is a desire on the part of many leaders to coach two or three things at once. This is almost always a disastrous coaching strategy. Work on improving the skill with the greatest leverage first. Do not try to coach your people or several skill areas at once. This will lead to confusion and frustration on both sides. Pick one and make real progress. Then, move on down the highway to the next one.

5. Beware of the "power of the poison pen." The best coaching is verbal and every day. Once you start to put coaching comments in writing on a regular basis outside of the formal review process, it will almost always

backfire. Never coach by e-mail or other forms of written communication. Do it face-to-face and only put something in writing as a very last resort. Coaching meetings in writing are viewed as a threat by employees. Once you put it in writing, your coaching contract with your employee becomes much more formal and trust erodes quickly.

Mentor Your People (As Individuals)

Mentoring your associates as a leader goes far beyond coaching and creating emotional connections. Are you aggressively advocating your people for positions of growing responsibility throughout your organization? Do you think of what is best for the company as a whole and your employees or do you focus only on what is best for your team, division and location? Leaders who are true mentors to their employees have a strong relationship defined across the following dimensions:

1. The employee clearly understands what is expected of them to deliver a superior performance.
2. The employee can say anything to their leader without fear of retribution.
3. The mentoring leader will meet with and visit with the employee anytime that it is important to the associate.
4. The leader has a personal accountability in his or her performance objectives for the future development and retention of the employee.
5. The mentoring leader shares openly with the associate what they need to do to get better every day.
6. The leader openly advocates moving qualified team members to positions of increasing responsibility both inside and outside of their organization.
7. The mentoring leader gives open feedback – both positive and negative - to the employee about how other people throughout the organization feel about them and why.
8. There is an emotional connection based on trust and caring about the welfare of each other.

The truth is, most companies give "lip service" to mentoring. I continually hear companies say we already have a mentoring program. However, when I ask whether or not mentoring key individuals in their organization is included in their personal performance objectives and compensation measure, most of the time they look down at their shoe tops. There is a huge difference between a real mentoring program and one that is for public consumption only. A mentoring program with teeth is when the loss of a top performing associate has a direct impact on the future of their leader within the organization. Mentoring programs, when properly designed and executed, can be one of the very best retention devices.

Invest in Development

Look for development opportunities outside your organization to develop your people. Recommend and place them on high priority initiative teams. In addition, send your folks to leadership development training where they will directly interact with people outside their industry. The more I speak and consult across industries, the more convinced I am that 98 percent of the business issues are the same. They revolve around customer challenges, team building, need for more innovation, the opportunity for two-way communication and the desire to control costs as well as increase profitability. These issues exist in the restaurant business, agriculture, engineering, energy, retail, telecommunications and countless others. Your people will benefit greatly by interacting with like professionals in other industries. They will have an appreciation that the problems they are experiencing are not unique to their business. In addition, it helps them take off their blinders and see the world much more broadly. This perspective will help improve their creative problem solving.

Strong Practical Growth Leaders expose their people to high visibility teams inside the organization and critical outside thinking by having them work periodically with talent from other industries to help bring forward a broader perspective.

Create an Associate Focused Culture (Words Matter)

Building an associate focused culture is a key and often overlooked retention device. Many of these initiatives do not cost anything. For example, do you address your people as employees or associates? More companies are increasingly using the term associates. I prefer the term associates because it recognizes the partnership we must all have to win together. This is an example of a culture focused on the needs of our people. What we call our people sends a clear message about how we feel about them. Think about it! Calling people employees sounds very "old school" and very transactional. Employees are people we pay to provide goods and services to drive the business. It is not a small distinction. Consider changing the term employees to associates today if you have not already done so.

Do you have two-way communication vehicles that make associates feel like they have a say upfront before key decisions are made by top management? Do decisions simply get handed down to the rest of the organization? Do you have real company town halls that are real attempts to gain input rather than "big tent" shows that are intended only to merchandise your decisions?

Consider outlawing management control words like staff. The management staff should be dropped in favor of leadership team. A manager is about control. A leader is about unlocking new possibilities. A staff is a management group focused on their individual divisions. A team supports each other and focuses on the common goal of winning together. This is not semantics . . . this is an attitude and a leadership mindset.

Do you have a comprehensive plan to on-board new associates for the first six months of their employment? An associate focused culture assigns a peer mentor beyond the boss to help support the new associate training and help them get acclimated to a new company culture.

Succession Planning Feedback to All Associates

Succession planning is the dirty little secret in business. It is the giant "black box" usually orchestrated by Human Resources and kept highly confidential from almost everyone. Succession planning defines the best candidates for potential future openings and highlights the candidates that are at various stages of readiness to assume different roles in the future. The process also usually includes a development component that focuses on what additional blocks of experiences various candidates need to make the move to the next level of the organization.

Practical Growth Leaders will win if they share this information more openly with their associates. Everyone already knows succession planning happens, but they are usually unaware of the discussions or decisions made as a result. A high performance culture is created only when everyone knows where they stand. Leaders fear doing this because they want to avoid making promises to top performers and saying anything that would cause average achievers to overreact. Therefore, it is too risky to share any meaningful succession information with associates. When you fail to tell people what is happening, they usually assume that the most negative possible scenario will take place. There are many times I have had clients who had a candidate ranked near the top in succession planning only to lose them a few months later due to the mixed signals sent by their manager.

Lead By Example in the Field

Lead by example by circulating as often as possible with the people on the front-line of the business. Take your people with you into the field when you go. There is a no more effective way to build emotional connections with your team than by going on a "field trip" together into the "line of fire" to learn about what is happening in your business. It is a great environment to travel together and strengthen your relationship together while building trust along the way. You can also work with the associate to build a joint action plan on what you will each do differently as a result of this new learning. It is important that these trips build your relationship together and are not used as finger-pointing exercises about what the associate can do differently. Utilize the "coaching every day" techniques outlined earlier in this chapter to keep the sessions positive.

Clearly Define Job Expectations

Every job does in fact need a job description outlining deliverables and expectations. I hate to write job descriptions. It can be tedious and boring. However, it is very necessary to clearly outline what the expectations are going into the assignment. This document (hopefully one page, maximum) gives you some objectives to go back to when there are different opinions about the dimensions and accountabilities of the job. However, job descriptions are not all inclusive of the requirements. It is a guideline only. This is important because job descriptions have endured a lot of bad press in recent years. Have you ever heard the comment, "That is not in my job description." That response can fall under the phrase, "...other duties as assigned." That is the standard catch-all phrase at the end of each job description. If you truly build emotional connections as a leader by building trust with your team members, you will never need to pull out a job description. Unfortunately, almost no one enjoys 100 percent success in building emotional connections with their people.

Highlight the Financial Value

It is important to remind associates of the total value you are bringing to the table financially. It is critical that you periodically reinforce this to your associates. This would include the following compensation benefit statement:

- Salary
- Bonus
- 401K
- Profit Sharing (if applicable)
- Benefits (cost if purchased on the open market)
- Perks with financial value
- Other

Total Dollar Value of Relationship

Do you have a one page statement that reinforces the individual and collective value of these benefits to your associates? People often only look at salary as the primary measuring stick to compare two employment offers. This intervention is necessary to make sure they consider the total value of their relationship with the company. While this information will not create new emotional connections, it can create a barrier if it is not periodically reinforced.

Building the Retention Momentum Bridge

The stakes are too high not to build the Retention Momentum Bridge. There will be a total shortage of top leadership talent in the coming years. At the end of the day, the building blocks of the Retention Momentum Bridge, combined with practicing the 8 Cs of leadership behaviors through emotional connections, provides a roadmap for retention that will lead you and your organization to victory. It will be very hard work and it will take a great deal of leadership time. However, it is much better to invest your resources upfront to retain your top talent than to chase new talent every day just trying to keep pace with the departure of your best people. The Practical Growth Leader that retains the best people over time is well positioned to achieve sustainable growth. The leader that fails to retain their best people will be stuck in neutral on the mature side of the growth curve.

Hiring the Best People

What are the characteristics to look for when you are hiring the best people? Most companies have interview processes to try to answer that, along with elaborate evaluation tools and testing criteria (in some cases) to try to evaluate candidates against key success measures.

Some very wise leaders, who I once worked with, told me about the five things you need to evaluate when you are deciding whether or not to hire someone:

1. Are they smart?
2. Do they work hard?
3. Can you trust them?
4. Do they have a positive attitude and a passion for winning?
5. Do they have a past track record of results that can predict future behavior?

Smart

As hard as I have tried my entire career to do it, I have never been able to teach someone how to be smart. You can train them how to do the job, but you cannot increase their raw intelligence. We talked about Hi/Low leaders in Step 1. These are the rarest leaders who can fly at 50,000 feet developing strategy and also glide just above the tree tops because of their granular knowledge of the business. Put evaluations in place to find these people and you will grow your business. Unfortunately, the business world is full of strategic leaders who cannot execute anything. The world is also full of people who can execute and deliver anything as long as you tell them what to do. The key is to find leaders who understand how to develop a strategy as well as how to bring it alive in implementation. As Hannibal Smith (played by George Peppard), the gruff leader of "The A Team" used to say, as he chewed on a cigar, "I love it when a plan comes together." Find and hire leaders that can both develop the plan and make it come together with flawless execution.

Work Hard

I have also tried throughout my career to motivate people to work harder. In the end, you can create a motivating environment to work hard, but the decision to do it is ultimately not yours to make. It is critical for you to determine someone's work ethic prior to hiring the person. The other critical point here: do not measure work ethic only by the hours worked in an office setting. Most leadership roles allow for working at home and on location where the business is happening. In the end, only results count! In your opinion, is this person smart enough and do they have the commitment level necessary to deliver results?

Trust

You cannot train someone to be trusted at work. The world is full of unsuccessful leaders who deliver results, but cannot be trusted. The recent corporate scandals across several industries with top corporate leaders duping their employees and shareholders and winding up in jail are real world examples about the scarcity of trust. Trust builds relationships and motivates teams to work together. A lack of trust is a relationship killer. So, if trust is so important, how do you measure whether or not a person has this critical characteristic? There are three critical techniques to measure trust during the selection process:

1. Ask other leaders to interview the same candidate to measure consistency. Pick three critical questions and make sure everyone asks them exactly the same way. In a post-interview group meeting with the other leaders, determine whether or not the answers were consistent. If the answers vary significantly to any of the three pre-selected critical questions, chances are you have a trust issue on the table.

2. Ask the candidate if you can contact the people who have worked for them earlier in their career as well as peers to talk about what they are like to work for, and with, every day. If they refuse to offer up any names (not counting their current employer), that tells you a great deal about them from a trust standpoint. If they do offer names, call the people and listen carefully to what they say and don't say about the candidate as a leader.

3. Have a top leadership candidate interview with front-line employees including administrative assistants. Do they treat front-line employees with the same degree of respect and value them as much as the top leaders in the organization? Front-line associate interviews can be very revealing about how the candidate is likely to treat everyone on the team and in the organization once they come on board.

Attitude

Positive energy is contagious. Why are people drawn to leaders who believe in the future possibilities of the business? There is nothing more powerful than a leader who has a clear vision, brings it alive through implementation and makes their people believe that in the end they will all win together.

Negative energy is also contagious. A negative leader sucks the energy right out of the team and organization. A negative leader often behaves like a Building Inspector, Bad News Employee or Painful Porcupine. A negative leader can kill growth.

Winston Churchill said, "Attitude is a little thing that makes a big difference." It is a crucial choice that every leader makes every day. As we stated in Step 1, energy and passion are free. Make a choice to bring them to work with you every day. It is critical that the leaders on your team make that same commitment.

Past Track Record – Future Predictor

Ask the candidate to outline past results they have achieved and how they did it. It is important to learn whether they achieved these results by steamrolling through the organization, leaving bodies in the hallways, or by being great collaborators who also built relationships that proved to be sustainable. If it is the former, it will be very difficult for the leader to be successful in most organizations over the long run.

In addition to hiring the right people, it is vital to recruit and retain the very best from each individual generation going forward. This will require the Practical Growth Leader to emotionally connect in new ways within and across the generations. The impact of these generational differences in the workplace is growing rapidly. I see sparks fly every day when I conduct generational workshop sessions for many Fortune 500 companies. It is the No. 1 topic I am asked to speak about and will continue to be for many years.

Cross-Generational Emotional Connections

Millennials

It is critical that Practical Growth Leaders understand the critical leadership differences across the generations. Understanding these differences is critical to winning the battle for top talent and leading diverse teams to victory. It is also a critical tool to help find, acquire and retain the best leaders in each generation. It is important to understand the unique perspective of the Millennial Generation.

The Millennial Generation (born 1978-2000) experienced Princess Diana, the Gulf War, the Oklahoma City bombing, Columbine, www., cell phones, 9/11, computer games and lived in a child focused world. To this group the Kennedy tragedy was a plane crash and not an assassination. They have always had pin numbers and made their purchases through scanners. They do not remember much about life before on-line. Google has always been a verb. Laptops have always fit into backpacks. The presidency has always been about someone named Bush or Clinton. NASA has experienced as many failures as successes. Schools are no longer a safe haven for children. A Tab is the heading on a computer file and not a diet drink. This generation values social consciousness, intellectual problem solving, teamwork, holistic lifestyle, ("work is only part of life"), technology dependence, respect for diversity and the achievement of goals. This generation was raised by the "helicopter parents" who hovered like choppers around their kids and gave them constant feedback and support. They have little long-term loyalty to any music artist or style, and tend to feel the same way about the companies they work for every day. Beloit College offers a powerful summary of the unique and changing perspectives of the Millennial Generation.

Millennials tend to school like fish. You will see them hang out together both during and after work. This will sometimes offend your older team members. Do not take the lack of inclusion as a negative. They tend to have unrealistic expectations about the need to "pay their dues" prior to the next promotion. They also tend to think that repeating the same activity over and over again is beneath them. This can be a challenge. Think about it! How many activities in any job are repeated every week or at least every quarter? This is the first generation that made lists of goals and activities beginning in elementary school. This is a positive relative to a Millennial being goal oriented. My only goal in elementary school was to make it to recess! They can also become restless more quickly to move on to the next thing on the list as they cross-off their accomplishments.

What does all of this mean to the Practical Growth Leaders? You must recruit the best from this generation by emphasizing work/life balance, appealing directly to their key influencers (including parents and significant others) and by emotionally connecting Millennials to the higher level mission of your industry. When you lead Millennials, you must also provide them with a dynamic team environment that is collaborative, encouraging and rewarding.

As a leader, you must also provide frequent performance feedback and support to Millennials. I am a Baby Boomer (I was born in 1954). If I got a performance review from my boss in January, and received no raise until August, no problem. I would see my boss in the hallway and smile. Life was good! This will not be the case with Millennial Generation. You must give supportive ongoing feedback individually - just like the "helicopter parents" - and recognition publicly to this generation. If you do not, they will leave you. If three weeks go by and they haven't heard from you, they assume something is wrong. This generation will join you optimistic about the future and the role they will play in shaping it.

Generation Xers

Generation Xers (born 1965-1977) experienced the energy crisis, PCs, the Reagan era, VCRs, cable television, the Berlin Wall, Challenger and MTV. They were the first generation that learned their ABCs from "Sesame Street." Many of them grew up daily with single parents or families where both mom and dad worked outside of the home. They are self reliant and value building their skill portfolio. They grew up during the broad availability of cable TV and VCRs. Often career discussions with a Gen-Xer tend to feel like a negotiation. They tend to be unimpressed with authority and less loyal. They saw their parents go through downsizing and layoffs. They have a high degree of skepticism (high smoke meter detector) and they work to live, not live to work. Gen-Xers love adventure. They are more likely to get married on St. Thomas Island than their parents' church. Gen-Xers can appear more aloof. They appreciate the direct approach on an individual basis from their boss. They value technology and a wide range of assignments. They are pragmatic. Gen-Xers are much less likely to buy into doing something "for the good of the team."

In order to recruit and retain Generation Xers, Practical Growth Leaders must convince them that their assignment will build their skill portfolio, and communicate clear goals as well as expectations. Gen-X leaders will expect frequent as well as candid communication on how the team's growth initiatives are doing including the good, bad, and ugly. If you fail to link the assignments to building their skill portfolios, Generation X leaders will leave you for greener pastures.

Baby Boomers

Baby Boomers (born 1946-1964) are the parents of today's youth. They experienced the Vietnam War, Watergate, the Kennedy assassination, the first moon landing, the Beatles, Elvis, color television (including TV shows like "Mickey Mouse," "Star Trek," "The Andy Griffith Show" and "Happy Days") and the 1960s civil rights movement. Baby Boomers took long vacations in their family cars. Most of us grew up watching three or four television channels and going to drive-in movie theatres on Saturday night. Our computer experience began with a stack of punch cards and learning how to feed them into a large "Whopper" computer similar to the one that filled an entire room which was programmed by Professor Faulken in the 1983 movie, "War Games."

Baby Boomers live to work, are more willing to relocate, are goal attainment focused, team oriented, redefine everything and have a strong social consciousness. Baby Boomers will also be more title and status conscious than the other generations. Baby Boomers, above all else, want to make a difference. Whenever I give a speech about generational leadership, I ask each generation to stand up one at a time and cheer each other. The Baby Boomers are almost always the only generation that cheers for themselves. I think that is great! This generation lives to work and struggles with work/life balance. Baby Boomers like to be at the center of the stage with big ideas and believe in team building. They are more likely to take on projects with significant risk and can at times charge into a problem and get way over their heads.

Recruiting and retaining Baby Boomers will require a focus on how they will make a difference and contribute to overall team success. You will need to make sure Baby Boomer associates have solid goals that encourage them to focus their resources where they believe they will make the biggest contribution to growth. Also, be mindful of this generation's status attachment to titles and position within your growth organization. Creating an environment that encourages and rewards knowledge transfer will be critical to the organization as Baby Boomers transition toward retirement. Baby Boomers tend to talk in terms of a general high level management style, but practice a more detailed hands-on style which can at times be viewed as controlling by Gen-Xers and Millennials. Give Baby Boomers recognition for their work ethic, long hours and most of all results.

Baby Boomer Trap

We will share a Baby Boomer Golden Growth Segment example in Chapter 4 that points out the significant risk of lumping Baby Boomers into one large group. The fact is there are major life experience differences between early and late Baby Boomers. This will be highlighted where we introduce a fifth generation known as Generation Jones. This will be defined as a separate and distinctive generation. This is the most wealthy and powerful generation of all from a marketing and change standpoint. Stay tuned for a new awakening of how to grow your business across generations.

Traditionalists

Traditionalists (born before 1946) experienced the great depression, FDR's New Deal, World War II, D-Day and the atomic age. They have strong values for boundaries, duty, honor, security and life-long careers. They believe very strongly in loyalty, hierarchy, respect for authority, conformity and discipline. To recruit and retain traditionalist employees, Practical Growth Leaders must reinforce the value they are contributing, emphasizing their direct contributions to profitable revenue growth. It will be critical to enlist traditionalists as mentors to younger generations. Some of the very best growth mentors in many organizations are traditionalist leaders. Again, knowledge transfer incentives will be critical as this generation transitions toward retirement.

Synergizing Across Generations

There are several key points to emphasize regarding cross-generational leadership. The goal is to find, recruit, as well as retain the very best Practical Growth Leaders and innovators from each generation to your team. In addition, you must find the right rhythm and cadence to motivate each generation. For example, Millennials will view your industry as far more desirable if you emotionally connect with a higher mission focused on the greater good your business contributes to society as a whole. Generation X team members will feel a special connection to their leader when you show them how you are building their skill set portfolio to support their personal development. Baby Boomers must know above all else that they are personally making a difference every day. Traditionalists will be very focused on their top line and bottom line contribution. The really good news is that if you utilize the 8 Cs of The Practical Growth Leader, you will be well positioned to motivate and leverage synergy across the generations. All the generations will respond positively together to peacetime praise, flexible work schedules, and clear communication on goal setting as well as progress to date vs. objectives. Caring, Candor, Confronting Conflict, Circle of Trust, Collaboration, Credit to Others, Communication and Celebration properly applied to each group represent a clear path toward creating a powerful growth culture.

Diversity Growth Engine

It is also important to keep in mind that cross-generational leadership is only one aspect of diversity. There are many other aspects of diversity to consider when building a growth team including people of color, gender and style. The cross-generational aspect of diversity is highlighted here to raise Practical Growth Leader sensitivity to the different life experience and perspective variables one must consider when leading a growth team. The most important thing to remember is that the most ineffective growth team is populated with team members that look alike, sound alike, have the same thought process, same strengths and similar style that you have as a Practical Growth Leader. The real and sustainable team growth model is fueled by diversity that cuts across all of these dimensions. Think about a great basketball team. It is made up of two lightning-quick guards – one of whom can handle the ball with the deftness of a magician – a power forward, a shooting forward and a towering center. You don't want to field a team of five 7-foot centers or you're in for a long night.

To recruit and retain highly diverse teams, an insightful Practical Growth Leader must create and communicate the higher mission the business represents for the betterment of society and the global community.

Emotionally Connect to Your Industry

What business are you really in going forward? In order to recruit, retain and motivate employees, you must convince them that your industry creates the best working environment. In order to do this effectively, you must ladder up to a higher emotional connection. Why should your team come to work every day? Here is a hint. The correct answer is not a pay check. This will be critical to the Millennial Generation and important to every practical growth team member. Most companies tend to define themselves by function or product category. They fail to make an emotional connection between their company's mission and the reason their employees come to work every day.

Agriculture represents a great example of an industry that has the potential to make a stronger emotional connection with its employees. This industry, like many others, is faced with a severe workforce shortage in the next five years as Baby Boomers retire. As these leaders are replaced by the Millennial Generation, the need to create a higher level emotional connection will become even more important. The following chart highlights how to emotionally connect agriculture in a new way with Millennials, who may consider joining the industry.

Top Five Reasons Agriculture is the Very Best Industry
(Example of Laddering Up)

1. Agriculture helps create and nurture relationships	The book "Never Eat Alone" Every time you eat alone, you miss the opportunity to build a relationship
2. Agriculture brings families together for meals	Research concerning the family bond of eating together
3. Agriculture helps provide healthy and well balanced food choices	Fitness and wellness is growing and sustainable trends
4. We Feed The World	During difficult times in the world, one industry steps forward to help
5. Agriculture combines technology with the need to provide for people	Technology advances are critical to recruiting top people outside of agriculture

This agriculture example is not unique. It is critical to create a higher emotional connection to recruit in all industries including health care, insurance, financial, manufacturing, retail, restaurants and many others. How would you create a powerful emotional connection to your company? Your future growth will depend, in part, on doing it successfully. If you make an emotional connection between your company and your employees, you are much more likely to win the battle for talent.

Summary

Hiring and retaining the right people up front will help you build a winning team. If you miss on a top leadership hire, it can take years to recover. By answering the five questions outlined in this section, you will go a long way toward picking Practical Growth Leaders who can drive your business. Try to get past the façade put up as a force field by the candidate and find ways to look into their souls as leaders and as people.

Practical Growth Leaders play to win by recruiting and retaining the best innovators across each generation to their team. Leaders also understand that marketing and selling your company to recruits is migrating from the cold call by an uninvited guest to creating new emotional connections with your company and industry. Your ability to emotionally connect your team to the industry you are living in together every day will be a key to recruiting and retaining the very best.

What's Next?

Finally, in the end, it always comes down to relationships. Speaking of relationships, you will never have one more important than the emotional connections you create with your customers. It is often the deciding factor that determines whether or not you achieve your growth objectives. We now move on to Step 3 which is all about building customer loyalty every day.

Are you ready to clear the Step 2 hurdle?

Step 2 Hurdle Test

1. How does the people leadership role need to change?

2. What are the key components of the Retention Momentum Bridge?

3. Describe three examples of the unexpected caring leader.

4. What are the top five Practical Growth Leader coaching techniques?

5. Describe what a true leader mentoring program looks like.

6. What are the top five variables for Practical Growth Leaders to use in hiring team members?

90-Day Top Talent Flex Plan for Growth

Time Frame	Activities
30 Days	What coaching everyday plans do you and your team currently have in place?

What elements of the "Retention Momentum Bridge" are in place and where are your gaps?

60 Days   Build individual coaching everyday plans for Practical Growth Leaders throughout your organization.

What are three to five specific things each month you will do as an "unexpected" leader?

Complete a screen of your company's hiring process against the top five variables for selection.

90 Days   Refine and build a true mentoring program by assigning top executives to work with your highest potential Practical Growth Leaders at all levels of the organization.

Reevaluate how to integrate the Practical Growth Leader coaching everyday concept into your mid-year and year end performance reviews.

Conduct a cross-generational workshop with your team that highlights generational differences and how we can all win together across the generations. How would you "ladder up your industry" to a higher emotional connection to help you recruit and retain the very best people across each generation?

CHAPTER 3

Step 3: Pedal to the Metal – Customer Loyalty Now!

American educator and writer Peter Drucker said, "The purpose of business is to create and keep a customer." There are three major growth starters that will ultimately decide whether you win or lose the passionate pursuit to grow your business. They are the fuel in the tank of your growth engine.

1. Growing customer loyalty
2. Creating innovation flight plans
3. Finding fast competitive passing zones

These three growth starters will be reviewed in detail over the course of the next three chapters. Growing the business always begins with the customer. We will review how to leverage Customer as Family, Real Time Measures, Front-Line Employees (Employer Branding), Peacetime Customer Interviews and Value Creation Relationships to build customer loyalty every day.

Growing Customer Loyalty

The simple truth is most companies don't know how to grow customer loyalty over time. What is happening with your customer loyalty momentum? Put another way - are your customers more or less loyal than they were 90 days ago and why? How do your customers experience your brand and company every day? Customer service is eroding to a crisis level. Based on a poll of more than 8,600 customers responding to a recent survey by BIG Research for the National Retail Federation and American Express, 85 percent of customers believe service is staying the same or getting worse over time. Almost 50 percent said it is getting worse.

That's certainly not the case at one of the most popular family-owned restaurants in the Midwest.

Where the Customer is Treated Like Family

It was a beautiful Midwest Sunday afternoon in sun-drenched Independence, Missouri.

The line of customers at the Tim's Pizza counter extended out the door and onto the sidewalk of the iconic eatery, which has become a favorite of everyone from bank presidents and mail carriers to former big league ballplayers and high school sweeties on their first prom date.

Standing near the pizza oven, loading a house special with all the ingredients that make it the most popular pie this side of the Mississippi, is co-owner Tim Pace.

He's soon approached by a gentleman who owns a shop in the same strip mall that has been the home of Tim's Pizza's for the past 19 years. He says, "You have to be nuts! It's a great day, it's Sunday – and you're here doing something you could be paying a kid $5 bucks an hour to do."

Pace grins, and asks what he'd like on his pizza.

"If I'd have had that attitude when we opened this place," Pace, 52, said, "I doubt if we'd still be here."

Tim's Pizza is a place where the customer is No. 1.

As soon as a regular pulls into the parking lot, Tim or his brother, Steve, 46, have a drink on the counter and a copy of the afternoon paper awaiting their arrival.

"The guys are amazing," said former Kansas City Royals catcher Brent Mayne. "I had a friend visit from California and we had the house special. It was great, but Steve noticed my friend took off the green peppers and put them on the side of the plate.

"When my friend came back the next summer, we went to Tim's and Steve says, 'House special, no green peppers – right?'

"It blew us away."

That special treatment isn't just reserved for friends of major leaguers.

"If you go to Tim's," Allen Lefko, the president of the Bank of Grain Valley, said, "you know your drink is going to be on the counter when you walk in the door and your pizza is going to perfect. It's been that way for 19 years."

One word – consistency – best sums up the Pace brothers' approach to business.

"We believe in consistency," Tim Pace said. "We know everyone by their first name, we know – and care - about their families and we usually know what they're going to order.

"We've been open 19 years and there hasn't been a day in those 19 years that Steve or I haven't been here greeting every customer."

And calling them by name.

Tim's Pizza hats have been spotted on nationally televised sporting events, cable news broadcasts and in photos that customers have sent from around the world.

There isn't a spot on the wall of their 3,600-square foot establishment that isn't covered by a thank you note, wedding or baby announcement or a hand-drawn piece of art from a class thanking them for donating a pizza for a special project.

Over the years, Tim's Pizza has sponsored more than 600 little league sports teams and the two likeable brothers are pace setters when it comes to making charitable contributions.

They don't conduct a news conference when they make a donation to a favorite charity; they do it for all the right reasons.

"We like to help," Tim said, "that's all. If someone needs help, and we know about it, we want to be there for them."

Their unique approach is one reason why the *Kansas City Business Journal* wrote that: "Tim's Pizza is recession proof."

"Someone once asked me how I know the name of every customer who comes into our place," said Steve, as he sorted through a huge box of green peppers, "and I just said, 'When someone comes in here and puts a $20 bill in my hand, I better remember their name.' The people who come in here on a regular basis aren't just customers, they're family."

In an age where mom and pop businesses disappear from the scene on a regular basis, Tim's continues to thrive.

"We won't talk about money," Tim said, "but about once a month someone comes in and asks if we'd like to sell the place or franchise it.

"But we're not interested in that. We've found our niche and we have some special individuals who have made this a success. We have wonderful employees (36-year-old Randal Stevenson has worked at Tim's most of the 19 years the doors have been opened) and people just know what to expect when they come to our place."

At one large table, a young couple celebrates their engagement vows. A mom is chasing down a 3-year-old, who wants to peer in the observation window to watch Tim or Steve put the final touch on another pizza masterpiece.

Another satisfied Tim's devotee takes one last look at the last bite of his taco pizza and pops it into his mouth with the look one often associates with spotting your favorite gift under the Christmas tree.

"We had a guy come in the other day and we'd never seen him before,"

Tim said, "so we asked where he was from."

The new customer said he was from Independence, but that he had just returned from Florida.

"He told us that while he was in Florida, he saw this guy wearing a Tim's Pizza hat," Tim said, chuckling. "He said he'd driven by our place 100 times, but had never stopped. He asked the guy wearing the hat down in Florida about us and he said, 'It's the greatest pizza place in the world.'"

The newcomer is now a familiar face at Tim's, where every pizza comes with the type of genuine smile that makes you feel at home.

There are at least three powerful marketing concepts at work that make Tim's Pizza a very unique success story. First of all, the "personal touch" of caring for the customers individually as people by remembering everything from their names, family members, interests, as well as knowing how to personalize their order. I am reminded of another successful establishment in Boston during the 1980s called "Cheers," "Where everybody knows your name."

Second, there is the "give/get" principle of marketing. The owner's involvement in sponsoring over 600 youth sports team is a wonderful way to give back to the community that has also had the multiplier effect of generating increased long-term customer loyalty of coaches, parents, grandparents, and the kids themselves as they grow up. Tim's Pizza did not sponsor all those teams just to increase customer loyalty; they did it because it was the right thing to do, and a way to give back to the community. The same can be said of their planned low visibility charity commitments. They "give" to their local community because it is the right thing to do, and not tied to any business results. This willingness to give unconditionally is rewarded by friendship and increased customer loyalty.

Third, they understand and practice what marketers call a brand activation device. That is what Tim's Pizza hats are all about. These fun hats, seen all over the place, activate their brand with new customers and reinforce the loyalty of current ones. It is a simple and powerful idea. The passion and energy generated by Tim's Pizza environment has also helped to retain the long-term loyalty of their best employees which has contributed to increasing customer loyalty. Tim's Pizza is a single restaurant. Never underestimate the power and creativity of a successful small business owner, especially one whose apron is covered with flour from the pizza dough he tossed that morning. In today's business environment, there is too much emphasis on the innovation initiatives being championed by large corporations. There should be more widespread recognition of the entrepreneurs who leverage their smaller size to create bigger ideas.

Real Time Measures

What is happening to your customer loyalty? How do you know if it is increasing or decreasing? Real time measurement is growing in importance because a company can get into trouble very quickly when it is headed in the wrong direction. More and more companies are moving toward two-way communication with customers based on new technologies that facilitate brand momentum measures and recovery plans in real time as fast as a new Millennial can upload an I-Pod. The stakes are too high to wait for 30 or 60 day recaps on customer loyalty measures reported back from the front-lines to the Board Room.

A great example of utilizing technology to provide real time feedback is a program called the "iNTouch Success Center." It is important to note that the Millennial Generation is coming into the workforce in droves with high expectations that you know how to communicate and interact with them in real time. I have personally visited with many clients about this new segment of the workforce. Many of them are or soon will be your clients and customers. They want responses to their questions in real time utilizing cutting edge technologies. You need to know how to interact with them via text message and how to join their on-line communities. I must confess that I was a late adopter to technology. However, now I take my laptop and hand held on-line capability wherever I go. In my business, there is no other option. The customers and clients I work with demand real time responses.

Winning Hearts on the Front Line

There is no other single factor that impacts your customer's loyalty more than your front-line employees. Why? They come in direct contact with your customers everyday. They are your company and brand. More importantly, the majority of these contacts will occur when you are not there. It stands to reason that the only way to grow customer loyalty over time is to win the hearts of your front-line employees.

Are your employees more or less loyal than they were 90 days ago? Just like any sports team, no one's performance ever stays the same. You are either getting better or getting worse. The same is true with customer loyalty. It is either growing or declining every day.

Customer loyalty is growing in importance as a topic across industries as more companies are faced with the need to grow customer loyalty utilizing limited resources. Companies are making substantial investments in marketing dollars attempting to build the loyalty of their customer base and acquire new business. The majority of these incentives are targeted directly toward financial rewards or national program communication plans to motivate customers with a call to action. What is the number one factor that impacts customer loyalty in both large and small companies? The bottom line is that your front-line employees who directly interact with your customers every day have the single largest impact on loyalty. Remember, as J.C. Penney said, "Every great business is built on friendship." Tim and Steve Pace, from Tim's Pizza, would say the same thing. Front-line employees know the customer best and are the key influencers in the customer buying decisions. While this is broadly accepted by business leaders, we continue to under-invest resources in improving front-line employees' attitudes, engagement and commitment toward the brand and the business.

Southwest Airlines Front-Line Employees Win Hearts

As I am writing about customer loyalty, I am on a Southwest Airlines Flight from Orange County, Calif., to Las Vegas. The flight attendant has just announced with great pride that Southwest Airlines takes delivery on a new plane every nine days and plans to do so over the next five years. Much has been written about the "lightning in a bottle" that Southwest Airlines created in the airline industry. What is so critical about this story from a customer standpoint is how this company transformed the entire value chain including the flying experience, created a passionate group of associates, reduced prices and improved timeliness.

I personally visited with the president of Southwest Airlines, Colleen Barrett, during a trip she made to Kansas City. I learned that she sent greeting cards to all of her employees recognizing their birthdays and other special occasions. She was utilizing the 8 Cs of the Practical Growth Leader beginning with caring about her employees. What a great story of building loyalty through caring about your employees and customers. It is also a story of building customer loyalty through simplifying the value chain and focusing only on what matters. Southwest Airlines reminds us that true loyalty is built by making your customers' lives better and emotionally connecting to your front-line employees.

The Southwest Airlines story is all about "helping" the customer. Why does Southwest only hire 3 percent of the people it interviews? It values team spirit and attitude above all else. My guess is that Southwest will employ a great deal of top talent from the Millennial Generation going forward. This is because they emphasize a positive attitude and ability to be a part of a top performance team. This is in the sweet spot for a Millennial because they grew up functioning on working teams beginning in elementary school. Southwest trains its people well on the details of running their operation. Their true competitive advantage is driven by making the employees number one and empowering them to help their customers.

Employer Branding Builds Customer Loyalty

Al Ries, a legendary marketing strategist and best selling author, once said, "What's your brand? If you can't answer that question about your own brand in two or three words, your brand is in trouble." How do you increase employee engagement and commitment? How do you win the hearts of your front-line employees, resulting in building and sustaining customer loyalty? As pointed out earlier in this book, the biggest decisions in life are emotional. The benefit of employer branding is that it creates a powerful emotional connection between the leadership of the company and the front-line employees. You must be able to describe your company's brand essence in three words or less to every front-line employee.

The Brand Flag

As part of our employer branding initiative at Hallmark, we introduced a brand flag that had the name of every employee in the company printed on the Hallmark flag. The flag was permanently displayed at Hallmark headquarters. I remember seeing a young twenty-something woman proudly showing her parents her name on the flag when they visited our headquarters. I would also see fathers and mothers show their kids their name on the Hallmark flag. This took place all the time. It's like winning a championship in high school or college and going back to the gym and proudly showing a family member your name on a banner. The brand flag became a symbol for employees and their connection to the company. What if you have several locations? You can reproduce the flag for each location with a special spotlight or highlighter for the employees' names featured.

How did we handle the logistics of the flag when employees left the company? A new, revised version of the flag was produced every January with updated employee names to kick-off the New Year. It was one of the wisest investments we ever made.

Beliefs and Values

Do your employees embrace your brand beliefs and values? Roy Spence of GSD&M is an impressive leader and marketer. Spence is the president of GSD&M which is an agency in Austin, Texas that offers a creative, energizing and interactive culture. During my first visit to GSD&M, Spence took us on a tour of the agency. The beliefs and values of the agency were engraved in concrete in the foyer of the building. I listened to him talk about the beliefs and values of GSD&M from his heart as he walked us through their building. I was struck by the impact of having your company's beliefs and values permanently positioned and interwoven into your culture and building. Where do you keep your beliefs and values? Do you have them in public view throughout your company in a permanent position every day? Hallmark has its beliefs and values on the 5th floor for every supplier, customer, and employee to view when they walk by it. These are important symbols that reinforce the need to practice your values. The public display of your values represents your commitment to try to bring them to life everyday.

Heritage/Timeline

What is your company heritage and timeline? Do you have it displayed permanently so that employees know the history of how your company evolved into what it represents today? We built a corporate timeline that is permanently positioned inside our headquarters. This helps employees to connect emotionally with the history and heritage of the brand. As part of the employer brand display, there is even a cornerstone of the YMCA building where J.C. Hall stayed in 1910 when he first began to sell postcards out of a shoebox he kept under his bed. Where do you think the name "Shoebox Greetings" came from? This heritage will always be a critical part of what Hallmark is and what the Brand represents. What is your company heritage? Do you have a timeline on display for all your employees to see and understand your brand journey?

The ironic part of employer branding solutions such as brand flags, beliefs and values displays, timeline history and heritage story telling is that they don't cost a lot of money to implement. My experience is they work hard to create an emotional connection between your brand and front-line employees. These symbols take the emotional impact to a whole new level. Just like the emotional power created when Ronald Reagan said to Mikhail Gorbachev in 1987, "Tear down this wall," or when playing George Gipp in "Knute Rockne: All American," as he lay dying in bed he urged Coach Knute Rockne to tell his team to go out and, "Win one for the Gipper." These levels of emotion can also be created with your employees when you personally connect with them by using powerful brand symbols. Unfortunately, most companies fail to see the power of what they have right in front of them. Emotionally connecting employees to what your company stands for is the best retention technique of all.

The Brand Celebration

Do you celebrate your company and brand? Do you have a single time during the year that your company elevates the brand and celebrates its own special niche? Do you have a Brand Super Bowl Week? At Hallmark, we had Brand Week once a year in October to celebrate the brand and who we are. All employees were invited to participate in this event. The event included brand rallies, wearing brand colors and attire as well as the introduction of the new Crown Gallery space that included brand values, timeline, heritage and our beliefs and values. We also had Brand Friday, the first Friday of each month when employees wear brand colors and attire. The Hallmark brand is more than a logo. Those words mean a great deal to Hallmark employees. Hallmarkers know their brand essence is enriching lives. It's like being a part of a winning sports team. You don't see many letter jackets on players from a 0-10 team, but every member of a championship team wants to wear their school brand, or colors, following that successful campaign.

Are you creating an emotional connection between your employees and your brand? Where does the journey begin? How do you know where to focus your resources? Can you ladder up your emotional connections to win on the front lines? Every brand and company needs to celebrate more with its employees. There is no better way to celebrate your brand than storytelling about the key accomplishments and behaviors you want your team to model in the marketplace with your customers and clients. Celebrations also build brand momentum and remind everyone of what we can accomplish together. I challenge you to acquire a reputation as a leader who celebrates your brand and company too much.

Building the Employer Branding Engine

If you don't know where you are going, any road will take you there. The voice of his 1960s generation, Bob Dylan sang, "The times, they are a changin'." What has changed about your brand? It begins with an independent 360 degree evaluation of your employer brand. The 360 degree approach assesses your company's strengths and weaknesses (gaps) from an employee perspective across several company/brand dimensions including:

- Your mission statement that defines why you exist
- The beliefs and values – representing the core of the company
- The brand essence – two to three words that breath life into your brand
- Brand promise – Your brand agreement with the customer
- Brand momentum – Your customer loyalty to your brand at any given moment
- Brand trust – The stored brand equity in the fuel tank you have with your customers
- Shared vision – What is the future direction of your company?
- Brand communication – Employee and customer brand touch points

The assessment will need to measure the overall employee attitudes, engagement and commitment to your company/brand as well as highlight any generational differences in brand attitudes (e.g. Baby Boomers, Gen-Xers, Millennials). The survey questions need to be tailored specifically to your company and employees to produce the most accurate result. This assessment cannot be a cookie cutter approach with common questions across companies and industries with relative rankings against key variables. Rather, this approach requires independent, in-depth, one-on-one, confidential interviews with front-line employees to understand the deeper employee insights and attitudes toward your brand. The critical inputs from these interviews are utilized to complete the 360 degree assessment of your brand.

Employer Brand Building

Employer brand building plans are created with specific roadmaps that address the strengths and weaknesses that are discovered in the independent, confidential, in-depth employee interviews. There is growing evidence that the most effective way to win front-line employees' hearts with your brand and increase customer loyalty is to make sure you have a shared and consistent view of reality and the future vision. This must be combined with engagement in order to Play to Win:

Concept 3.1

Play To Win Reality Concept

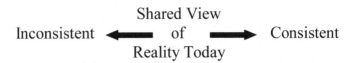

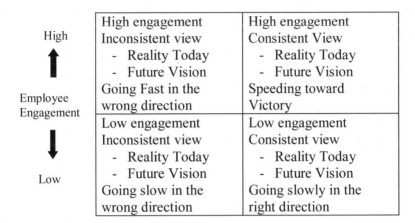

High engagement without a shared view of reality and a collective future vision can actually accelerate failure. Highly engaged employees going the wrong direction will fall off the cliff faster. The road to victory with employer branding should combine a high level of engagement with a clear and shared view of reality today, and a collective future vision. This is the rich soil that will grow future Practical Growth Leaders throughout your company. Leaders are the fuel that feed the growth engine. The best retention device you can create with your leaders is a clear and focused future vision, a common view of the brutal facts, and an unconditional belief in the power of your brand. As Ray Kroc, the driving force behind the golden arches of McDonald's said, "A brand for a company is like a reputation for a person. You earn reputation by trying to do hard things well."

Employee Relationship Plan

Once the collective view of reality and shared brand vision is clear to everyone, it is time to ignite engagement through a comprehensive employee relationship campaign.

What did John Kennedy, Ronald Reagan and Bill Clinton have in common? They were great campaigners who could emotionally connect with their audience. John Kennedy unlocked our imagination toward the future. Ronald Reagan was like a wise, reassuring grandfather. He reminded us of the greatness that is in all of us; that if we work together as a nation, we can win together.

Bill Clinton could reach out and show empathy to others in a way that made us feel like we would solve any problem together. Independent of your political views, these leaders connected with their vast audience. You need to be a great communicator with your customers and employees to be a true Practical Growth Leader.

What is your communication plan with your employees? It will be helpful if you think of it in the terms of a political campaign. The stakes are high and you must win their hearts. In the award-winning sitcom, "The Office," Michael Scott (played by Emmy winner Steve Carell) hosts an office party at which employees are given gold-plated trophies to reward them for their year's efforts. When one employee notices that the award is actually a bowling trophy, the flustered boss simply tells her to sit down, because, "They were out of the other trophies." How do you think she felt? Getting a six-inch trophy is bad enough, but getting a six-inch bowling trophy is inexcusable. The key difference between political campaigns and your employee communication plan is that you must deliver on all of your promises. Don't be like Robert Redford, the handsome young political newcomer from "The Candidate," who beat a much more experienced politician only to ask with a touch of desperation in his voice at the end of the film, "What do we do now?"

An employee relationship plan that consists of simple words, clear future vision, candor and consistent view of shared reality will drive up employee engagement. The employee relationship plan is designed to build an emotional connection utilizing a variety of communication tools, including two-way open forums, e-newsletters, magazine, e-mails and intranet. These relationship plans can be combined with interactive technology to facilitate real time communication between employees and the leadership team. You need to have a two-way employee relationship plan with specific ongoing forums where only two-way communication is on the agenda. When I was working with one of my clients on an employee-relationship plan, we determined that the best way to orchestrate two-way communication was to introduce "yellow cards," (rather than yellow challenge flags) that could be filled out by employees – signature optional – and sent directly to the leadership team to question anything happening in the company. This opened the two-way communication flow throughout the organization. Two-way communication is the best way to get involvement and engagement from the front line employees where the battle will ultimately be won or lost. You want to have a highly involved and engaged front-line team that also understands as well as embraces the shared vision. A strong employee relationship plan dramatically shortens the travel time and distance from the front-line to the board room.

The management team will need to be coached and embrace the 8 Cs of the Practical Growth Leader to make sure it can carry the brand Flag with front-line employees. If you fail to engage front-line employees effectively with your brand, you will erode customer loyalty over time.

Peacetime Customer Interviews

You can accelerate customer loyalty by conducting Peacetime Customer Interviews. Peacetime means you are not trying to sell them something during the interview. The time to build a relationship is when you can have an interaction when nothing big is at stake. It's like the distant relative who knows you have tickets to the playoffs, who calls and asks about the kids, the dog, the business and then finishes by saying, "And by the way, if you need someone to take to the playoff game, I'm available." He might have been a choice had he shown any interest in my family the dozen or so years I didn't have playoff tickets. Do you know what your customers believe to be the most important buying variable in your category? What are your strengths and weaknesses vs. competition?

These interviews can be well-positioned with customers. The positioning can be that great companies and partners want to get better every day. We want to continue our positive momentum to grow our business together.

The most critical point of Peacetime Customer Interviews is you cannot conduct them on your own. Do not do surgery on yourself in front of your best customers. An independent in-depth interview is critical because the customer will be less likely to try to leverage a third party independent interviewer. The process screens you from the customer, while at the same time, promotes more honesty. The customer will feel more comfortable talking with candor about your relative strengths and weaknesses if your company is not there. This will also help to avoid close relationships between key representatives of your company and the customer getting in the way of the good, bad and ugly assessment. Bill Gates of Microsoft once said, "Your most unhappy customers are your greatest source of learning."

The following in-depth qualitative questionnaire sample provides a road map that leads to success with your key customers. You might be tempted, but remember, don't try to perform surgery on yourself.

Independent In-depth Customer Interview
Peacetime Customer Interview Questions – Example

1. What is the number one strength our company has as your partner?

   How could we leverage this strength even more?

2. What is the number one weakness our company has as your partner?

   How should we address this weakness?

3. How would you rate our overall performance compared to our competitors?

High   Medium   Low

   Why?

4. In what areas do we have a clear advantage over our competition?

   Why?

5. In what areas do we have a sustainable disadvantage vs. other competitors?

   Why?

6. What three things should our company start doing to further strengthen our position with you as a customer?

   Why?

7. What three things should we stop doing to strengthen our position with you as a customer?

Why?

8. Has your customer loyalty to our brand changed over the past 12 months?

Increased   Stayed the Same   Decreased

Why?

9. What is the most important variable in your customer buying decision?

10. What is the critical factor that makes you choose or not choose our company?

Why?

11. If I could deliver one message to the people who run our company, what would it be?

Value Creation Relationships

What are you doing to create value for your customers every day and on every sales call? NFL Hall of Fame quarterback Roger Staubach, who starred for the Dallas Cowboys, said, "There are no traffic jams along the extra mile." As a former vice-president of sales, I would often ask senior sales leaders for their relationship plans. I would always challenge the relationship plan to make sure we had value creation for our customers. If you show me a company that only talks about the "great relationships" they have with their customers and not the ongoing value they are creating as their partners to drive their customers' business, I will show you a company that is about to lose business. The Peacetime Customer Interviews represent a great tool to take the customers' temperature about the value created in the relationship.

The Evolving Customer

The successful Practical Growth Leader understands that the selling model has evolved from selling to helping customers create value and solve problems. The balance of power has clearly shifted from the suppliers to the customers. The successful growth leader will create value for their customers by:

- Anticipating customer needs
- Knowing their customers' strengths and weaknesses
- Building trust
- Simplifying the customer value chain

Wal-Mart founder Sam Walton once said, "There is only one boss. The customer. And he can fire anybody in the company from the chairman on down, simply by spending his money elsewhere." That's a bold, but true, statement. How do you create value for customers? Do you bring forward new markets and products for your customers? Do you bring your customers in up front and early in your program development process? Are you sharing the changes taking place in your industry? Can you simplify and drive costs out of the value chain? Can you differentiate your customers' offering from their competitors?

The balance of power between clients/customers and suppliers has dramatically shifted in recent years. The days when annual golf events, dinners, and other customer perks will drive loyalty alone are long gone! That is not to demean these activities if they are a very small part of a value creation customer/client relationship. The days of keeping or acquiring business is no longer built on relationships alone. The tangible value creation your company brings forward to each of your key customers defines your true relationship. What are your value creation relationship plans with your customers? What is the cadence? Do you deliver value every two weeks or every two months? How do these variables compare with your competitors' value creation relationship customer model?

Summary

The bottom line is, to become a Practical Growth Leader, you must accelerate customer loyalty now. You must have a clear vision of how to accomplish your goal. For example, in the late 1800s, Marshall Field envisioned his store as a "Palace of desire," and described it as a place where you come through the front door and walk back out having to possess and buy something you did not know existed 10 minutes earlier. He also built his business around a powerful mantra that he called, "Give the lady what she wants." This became the front-line employee rallying cry during the early years of building the Marshall Field's brand.

The key starters to drive customer loyalty quickly are: treating the customer as family, winning with front-line employees through employer branding, Peacetime Customer Interviews and a value creation customer relationship plan. The customer perspective and power base has evolved, but in many ways business is still the same. It is still about anticipating and satisfying customer needs every day.

What's Next?

Now you are stockpiling Practical Growth Leaders faster than an effective college football recruiter. You are converting the Building Inspectors to leaders in front of the entire congregation, and you are replacing the Bad News Employees, Turtles Hiding in Their Shells, and Painful Porcupines, who refuse to change with more Practical Growth Leaders. Bravo! You are utilizing the 8 Cs of the Practical Growth Leader to create emotional connections to redefine your culture, and you are putting the pedal to the metal to jump start customer loyalty now!

We will now begin the journey to flex your Innovation Flight Plans. You will also learn how to find your PAC Power and chase the "gold segments." You will then move into the Fast Competitive Passing Zones with behaviors that will help you finish first.

Step 3 Hurdle Test

Kate Zabriske, a training industry expert, once said, "Although your customers won't love you if you give bad service, your competitors will." The choice in the end will be yours as a Practical Growth Leader.

Are you ready to clear the Step 3 hurdles?

1. What is your plan to ignite engagement with front-line employees?
2. Do you know how to develop an employer branding roadmap?
3. What are the benefits of an independent third party conducting your Peacetime Customer Interviews?
4. Do you have value creation customer relationship plans for your business?
5. Do you know how to measure your customer loyalty momentum in real time?

GROW NOW

If you answered these five questions with sufficiency, you can now take the fourth step of the eight steps to become A Practical Growth Leader.

90-Day Customer Loyalty Flex Plan for Growth

Time Frame	Activities
30 Days	Complete a 360 degree qualitative assessment inventory of how you and your organization measure customer loyalty.

– Is it real time?
– Do the measures being utilized "really matter"?
– Do the tools you are using focus on only the measures or the behaviors driving the outcomes?

60 Days	Utilizing the sample questionnaire in Step 3, develop a Peacetime Customer Interview survey that can be used for your industry and company.

Conduct a test of the Peacetime Customer Interview by beginning the first engagement with a small volume customer(s) to work out the issues prior to launching the new process to your larger customers.

90 Days	Conduct in-depth one-on-one interviews with key customers throughout your organizations identifying strengths and gaps directly against "what matters."

Conduct in-depth front-line employee interviews to determine whether or not they have a common shared vision and are engaged to achieve it for the common goal.

Build an Employer Brand plan that incorporates your brand symbols (e.g. flags), beliefs and values, brand promise, brand trust, heritage/timeline and brand/company celebration.

Build an employee relationship plan based on two-way communication and sharing feedback from Peacetime Customer Interviews and employee engagement perceptions around your shared vision.

Step 4: Flexing Innovation Flight Plans

Finding PAC Power – Leverage Strategic Advantage

Innovation is the high octane fuel of the Practical Growth Leader. Apple's Steve Jobs said, "Innovation distinguishes between a leader and a follower." Most change is incremental rather than transformational. How does real innovation happen? How do you achieve breakthrough and game changing growth, rather than incremental improvements?

Transformation change comes from finding your "PAC Power." What is "PAC Power?" It happens when permission exists to go to a new space that satisfies customer needs, combined with a unique capability to get there. It is defined as:

- Permission to move to a new space
- And
- Capabilities that can be uniquely leveraged to achieve a competitive advantage

Innovation Through Customer Permission

It starts with customer insights that reveal where they are willing to allow you to go as a brand. For example, it makes sense for an independent hardware retailer to offer a U-Haul rental service. Would that same retailer offer an expensive line of jewelry? Probably not. Pizza Hut offers hot wings with its pizza. How would customers react to Pizza Hut hamburgers? Think about it! They have the ground beef and distribution? But do they have permission? Innovation is an unpredictable and tricky business. Permission to move into new territory is not easily awarded to a brand and company.

Breakthroughs

Customers almost never come up with the ideas for breakthrough innovations, but they know them when they see them. Customers had no idea they needed Procter & Gamble's Swiffer cleaning products until they saw them and used them the first time. No one knew they had to have a My Starbucks cup of coffee every morning until they experienced it. How many pharmacy customers were clamoring for pharmacy drive-through windows until they were tested and introduced by industry leaders like Walgreens and others? These innovations represent game changers that successfully integrate customer permission and unique capabilities.

These game changers result from thinking just outside the chalk lines of your core business model. This PAC Power concept shows the Practical Growth Leader how to drive break-through thought creation rather than incremental improvements to the business.

Concept 4.1

Practical Growth PAC Power Concept
(Finding Permission And Capabilities Leverage)

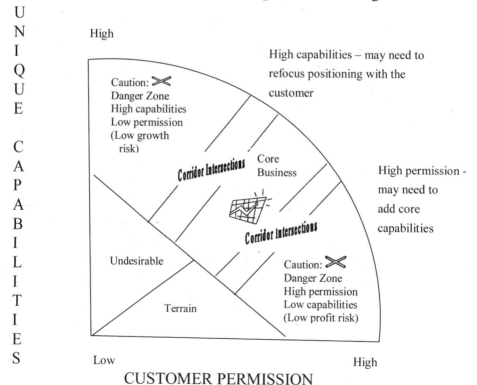

U
N
I
Q
U
E

C
A
P
A
B
I
L
I
T
I
E
S

High

High capabilities – may need to refocus positioning with the customer

Caution: Danger Zone High capabilities Low permission (Low growth risk)

Corridor Intersections

Core Business

High permission – may need to add core capabilities

Undesirable

Corridor Intersections

Caution: Danger Zone High permission Low capabilities (Low profit risk)

Terrain

Low

High

CUSTOMER PERMISSION

Growth Intersections

PAC Growth intersections are found most often in the corridors next to your core business. If you stray too far away from your core business, you will go to spaces customers will not give you permission to go or require capabilities you are unable to effectively acquire or create on your own. Finding these core growth corridor intersections is the key to providing real and sustainable growth. This concept illustrates that the greatest opportunity for growth usually lies in areas directly adjacent to your core business. When companies embrace aggressive growth objectives and go after unrelated businesses outside of their leadership team's core competencies, they are usually positioning themselves for a major fall. The only way to do this effectively is to acquire the capabilities through acquisition and/or strategic partnership. While this is certainly possible to do, history would say that the odds are not on your side. It is also usually much more difficult to make money consistently and provide an acceptable rate of return to shareholders when a significant portion of your portfolio lies far outside your leadership team's core capabilities. It is also important to emphasize that substantial growth opportunities reside in the heart of the core business.

Think of the heart of the core business like the reactor inside the Starship Enterprise space ship on the classic television series "Star Trek." The core business provides the fuel that makes everything else go. Many companies make the mistake of taking resources and focus away from their core businesses to chase after a new butterfly business that has much more excitement associated with it. Utilize the PAC Power concept to plant your innovation seeds in the most fertile soil. Put all of your innovation concepts through this assessment to determine how your core capabilities align with customer permission intersections.

Target Has PAC Power

In my opinion, Target is a brand and a retailer that understands PAC Power and how to leverage it very effectively to drive innovation in the marketplace. Target effectively leveraged its department store heritage to develop a strategy to appeal to a more affluent, female oriented guest. Target went after a more upscale taste level and married the concept of designers creating product for a value oriented retailer. This strategy grew over time as well as the loyalty of their more affluent and fashion forward guests. Target also values its associates' input into the innovation process. Target solicits input through "big idea" contests involving team members as well as outside expertise from design leaders, trend people, and movie and advertising people. This focus externally on the leading edge of the marketplace is why the Target logo has developed so much cache and loyalty among more affluent, fashion forward women. It is not the Target logo, but rather what it has grown to represent. A number of other rival retailers are moving quickly to try to catch up with the fast-break pace set by Target. It will not be easy to catch them. Target's rivals will be hard pressed to change the loyalty of these customers who have embraced what the Target brand represents. More importantly, these retailers will have difficulty competing with Target because fashion forward designing and partnerships are not part of their own PAC Power. The more affluent female customers are much less likely to give Target's rival retailers' brands the permission they need to effectively enter this space. It is not part of their brand heritage and current positioning. In addition, Target's rivals simply do not have the fashion forward, value capabilities that Target has worked so hard to develop over the past two decades. Target's biggest challenge is to develop the next series of innovation that will enhance their current position.

Fast Break Innovation Culture

How do you create a culture of innovation? You must recruit the innovative architects into your organization at all levels. You must create a culture that rewards calculated risk taking. In addition, your culture must be one of fast break speed. Your innovation offense needs to evolve around a "fast break" rather than a "grind it out" culture.

Legendary college football coach Knute Rockne was laughed at when he introduced this strange play called the forward pass. And when members of his backfield shifted to different positions before a play, opponents cried, "Foul!" Yet, during Rockne's 13-year coaching tenure, Notre Dame enjoyed five unbeaten and untied seasons. Rockne produced 20 first-team All-Americans and his lifetime winning percentage of .881 (105-12-5) still ranks at the top of the list for both college and professional football.

The man was an innovator. So, what specific culture changes are necessary to create fast-break innovation?

1. You Must Reward Risk-taking

This runs counter to the philosophy of most corporations. They are built for slow sustainable growth that carefully manages risk. These systems reduce surprises to shareholders and customers. Both of these groups hate surprises. They love and reward predictability. This high desire for predictability creates barriers to breakthrough growth. Most senior executives in corporations leverage the accountability word to manage risk. Accountability, in and of itself, is a critically important concept. As Ronald Reagan declared, "We must reject the idea that every time a law's broken, society is guilty rather than the lawbreaker. It is time to restore the American precept that each individual is accountable for his actions."

Leaders must be accountable to their growth and profitability objectives. However, this concept is too often misapplied to search for the guilty and punish risk takers within corporations. Many organizations misuse the word accountability to actually create more fear in their organizations. Nothing kills creativity and innovation faster than pumping the fear of making a mistake into the organization. You need to create an environment that rewards sound, calculated risk taking even when it does not bear fruit. The key to the reward of the risk is tied to the discipline of how the opportunity was framed up (pros and cons) and the quality of the business case. Practical Growth Leaders know that not every risk will pay off. They also clearly understand that there is a huge difference between well-calculated risk and one that was not well thought out. If someone continually takes risks that are not well thought out, they should be terminated and replaced as soon as possible.

2. Create Separate Innovative Organizations and Teams

One of the biggest mistakes organizations make is to charge the same leaders with both day-to-day business operations and achieving breakthrough growth through innovation. For example, Six Sigma, a quality and efficiency initiative that has been effectively utilized by companies such as General Electric, Allied Signal and Motorola, relies heavily on separate teams focused on specific measures. Likewise, the growth muscles needed to leverage innovation are very different from the ones most leaders use every day. If you charge the same leaders to manage and grow the business, you will likely see only incremental growth initiatives rather than breakthroughs.

By creating separate teams and organizations, you focus the company on the importance of growth. You create internal competition for the resources needed to grow. You break-down organizational layers and levels. You should create smaller organizations and teams that are housed in a different physical location, have very different looking calendars and furniture, and work at an accelerated speed. None of these dramatic cultural changes will happen if you charge the same leaders to grow the business incrementally and with breakthroughs. This is difficult for most Practical Growth Leaders to accept. It is a much easier path to have one leader in charge of a total category including day-to-day management and innovation.

Unfortunately, it rarely works. Why do you have very few professional football players play both offensive and defensive positions? It is because the mental approach to the game and skills needed are different between offense and defense at the professional level. On a rare occasion, a two-way performer like Deion Sanders will appear in the NFL, but most players are content with starring on one side of the ball. It is easier for football players to accept a one-sided role than it is for most business leaders. After all, innovation gets high visibility, top leadership focus and resources to fuel the growth engine. Players who try to play both offense and defense in football almost always lose focus as well as become less effective over the course of a season.

The same could be said about leaders who are attempting to run the daily operations of major businesses while attempting to achieve breakthrough growth at the same time.

3. Provide New Space for Innovation

Gen. George Patton said, "No great decision ever got made from a swivel chair." And he was right! Innovation should have a special and separate physical space in your company. The walls may look different. It could be a very different type of furniture housed in the innovation space. You must create an environment that fuels creativity and innovation every day. For example, the workplace shown in the hit movie "Office Space" in 1999 was an exaggerated view of the sterile environment of Corporate America. It would be hard to imagine an innovation team being lead by Bill Lumbergh (played by Gary Cole) achieving growth breakthroughs in the environment of the office depicted in the movie. If you integrate the people and talent needed to achieve breakthrough growth with the teams focused on driving the business every day, you will choke the innovative process. The day-to-day maintenance side of any sizable organization will absorb and cocoon around the innovation teams. Small and large companies alike underestimate the impact separate physical facilities have on your innovation culture. The environment should be constructed to fuel creative energy and growth. The best "space" to create an innovative atmosphere is with your customers in focus groups, retail stores and other forums where you can interact directly. Sam Walton built the largest retailer in America by spending almost all of his time in his stores. Work with your team to create a fun innovation zone in your company. It can have everything from basketball hoops to bicycles to swing sets to musical instruments to inspiring artwork. We first came in contact with many of these items for the first time as kids. It is widely recognized that children are much more creative than adults. As we grow older, our adult logical tendencies and practical focus begin to diminish our creativity. Surround your leaders with toys and watch them innovate. Some of the most creative and innovative ideas started in lofts, basements, farms, garages and cabins. Many of the greatest ideas that impact our life every day started in these types of locations, rather than in polished Madison Avenue offices. The importance of a physical location, with a separate team focused on innovation, are two critical variables that have a major impact on the organization's capability to deliver game changers. Pick a talented team and give them clear objectives as well as measurements to drive the business. Then, provide the team with the resources they need to win. Do not backfill their jobs and ask the rest of the organization to step up to pick up the slack. Finally, place the team in a highly creative physical environment and quickly get out of the way.

4. Test Small and Scale Fast

How do you effectively manage the risk associated with innovation? One of the most important aspects of innovation is to develop the capability to test small, directly and effectively managing the up-front risk. This is why a major retailer will make a test run before initiating a change in all its stores. For example, when chain drug stores, like Walgreens and CVS, introduced drive-thru pharmacies for the first time, it was tested first. What would be the operational issues? What was the impact on pharmacy sales? How did the drive-thru concept impact foot traffic and front-of-store sales? These are all logical and testable questions any leader would want to know the answers to before launching wide-scale.

It is important that the Practical Growth Leader carefully manage risk by testing small. This will increase the credibility of innovative initiatives in your organization, manage the up-front resource investment and increase the flexibility to change quickly, based on customer insights.

At the same time, the Practical Growth Leader knows that you also need to have the capability to scale fast into the marketplace in order to be first. The landscape is littered with companies that focused on testing new concepts only to be out-hustled to the broader marketplace by fast following competitors. The ability to scale large fast requires capital, investment capability and operational excellence. Combine those capabilities with innovation initiatives and you have a winning plan.

5. Develop the Winning Innovative Attitude

Winston Churchill once said, "Attitude is a little thing that makes a big difference." How do you create a winning innovation culture of confidence with swagger? It happens when you relate your success stories and celebrate failures. It happens when you take well calculated risks that many would say have no chance of success. That's right. By embracing the failures of well-calculated risks, you provide the best possible soil for planting the future seeds of innovation. A high energy, passionate, positive leader prepares the soil and plants the seeds for growth. A manager focused on control and "why it won't work" and who "to hold accountable" for mistakes sucks the life out of an innovation team.

Once you have created your growth corridor intersection, adjacent to your core business, as well as a fast-break innovative culture, it is time to focus on the who part of the question. Many companies commit to innovation and then focus their resources on mature or declining market segments to grow in order to enchance their business. It is much more effective to successfully establish your niche. Build it over time while you are chasing market segments that represent a slice of a pie - that is getting bigger every day. If you are only chasing shrinking pie market segments, you have little, if any margin for error. When you chase after Gold Growth Market segments, you are swimming with the downstream currents and going after the big fish. We will now examine two key distinctive Gold Growth Market segment case examples (Baby Boomers and women).

Chase Gold Growth Segments

The most important way to leverage your "PAC Power" (Permission And Capabilities) is to find and chase growth market segments. A powerful way to position your company or association for success is to go after the Gold Growth Segments and industries. These segments may be growing in population or influence or even purchasing power. If you focus on mature industries and market segments, you will usually wind up battling for a smaller share of a shrinking pie. If you focus on growth market segments, you are swimming with the currents and have a much better chance of achieving organic growth. There is a much better chance of finding gold through innovation when you focus on large segments that are growing purchasing power and influence. These intersections create points of leverage. We will now look at two case studies to illustrate Gold Growth Segments.

Baby Boomer Case Study

The following case study focuses on the impact of Baby Boomers (born 1946-1964) combined with their growing influence. It also highlights the need to carefully segment a customer group like Baby Boomers in order to maximize their market potential for your products and services.

There will be a huge market segment influence growing in importance over the next decade as Baby Boomers revolutionize their retirement golden years and extend or redefine their careers.

At 78 million people, Baby Boomers will represent the largest and most influential single constituency in the United States and the world. People older than 50 control over 70 percent of the total wealth (2.1 trillion of purchasing muscle) in this country - and we are not going away peacefully. Approximately 10,000 people turn 50 every day. Practical Growth Leaders who get ahead of the curve will lead the way. The financial community, led by companies such as Ameriprise Financial, Fidelity Investments, Wachovia, Lincoln Financial and Bank of America, are all targeting Baby Boomers through a variety of products, services, and advertising campaigns. The competition to manage Baby Boomer wealth is ongoing every day. Financial entities that resonate with their message stand to win big dividends. Baby Boomers will react strongly to financial messages that emotionally connect with their experiences.

Consider the impact of the aging Baby Boomers on health care. Companies like Bayer are introducing lines of nutritional supplements targeted at Baby Boomers. Major chain drug stores such as Walgreens, CVS and Longs represent strong retail distribution clearly focused on Baby Boomers. Wal-Mart and Costco are both emphasizing their pharmacy business to appeal to Baby Boomers. GNC targets Baby Boomers with a variety of "Gold" products focused on the over-50 market segment.

Packaged goods companies will also be targeting empty nester Boomers with smaller portion appetizers, entrées and desserts. For example, Sara Lee introduced a line of frozen pies six inches in diameter that will reduce or eliminate leftovers. General Mills, Quaker Oats and Kellogg's have introduced a number of natural cereals and lower cholesterol choices targeted toward Baby Boomers. Healthy choices will continue to escalate in the next decade.

Baby Boomers will want to age gracefully and stay youthful longer than any other generation before them. Beauty products for Boomers will continue to be the rage in the next decade. More products like Dove "Pro-Age," which are skin and hair products created for Baby Boomers, will be introduced at a rapid pace. Baby Boomers are like an aging professional football team. Just give them one more year and they will win the Super Bowl – they aren't getting older, they are getting better. That might be true for Denver Bronco quarterback John Elway, who retired clutching a Super Bowl championship trophy, but for most of us, it's only a dream.

Baby Boomers also represent the growing number of grandparents with a lot of disposable income to spend on grandkids. It is widely estimated in the toy business that grandparents account for 25 percent of all sales. This has major implications for companies like Fisher-Price and KB Toys. For example, KB Toys launched a grandparents' reward program.

Baby Boomers are the "do-it yourself" generation. This growing market segment will need more hardware stores. This positions chains like Home Depot, Lowes and independent hardware retailers to take advantage of this trend. It is important to note that Baby Boomers have a higher expectation going into a store than younger generations raised on the big box concept. Retailers who win the battle for Baby Boomers will combine a higher service level with distinctive choices targeted toward this generation. This plays well to retailers that place customer service at the top of their list.

Baby Boomers will be a great target for luxury products and vacation destinations over the next decade as they will begin to retire with more discretionary time and income. All-inclusive vacation resorts catering and pampering specifically to Baby Boomers will continue to grow in the coming years.

Madison Avenue Advertising View – Who's Hot?

The hot audience in advertising has always been the 25-to-49 age demographic with 20 percent to 40 percent premium cost on media. Everyone wants to chase the young and influential crowd. That's where future trends can be found. It's where the dollars are right now. It is where you can contemporize your brand. Unfortunately, none of these statements are really true anymore. It used to be somewhat true when the Baby Boomers were 25 to 49 years old. However, marketers and advertisers are beginning to wake up and realize the premium value of the Baby Boomer market. As Boomers age, their influence will continue to grow.

Baby Boomers have also gone on-line to find information and to make purchase decisions. The value of traditional media is declining rapidly as a way to reach this growing market segment. The generation that grew up as kids with three or maybe four channels can now surf over 300 channels on their television. Satellite radio and I-pods are replacing traditional AM/FM radios the way cassettes replaced 8-tracks in the 1970s. Newspaper readership continues to decline from 77 percent in 1970 to 50 percent or less today. On-line choices will become even more important to Baby Boomers in the future.

Millennial Boomer Influence

Baby Boomers are also key influencers to the Millennial generation (born 1978-2000). Millennials grew up in a more child centered world and have much closer relationships with their parents compared to prior generations. They are much more likely to rely on their Boomer parents to help make major purchase decisions. Marketers appealing to Millennials to make major future purchase decisions need to make sure they can cultivate Boomers as the key influencers to help close the sale. This "helicopter involvement," which involves a parent hovering over their kids, is not always positive. A placement director from a major university on the East Coast of the U.S. confided to me how a father impersonated his son during a first round telephone interview. He hoped to try to get his son through to the second round of the process, which involved personal face-to-face interaction. When the employer's recruiter discovered this technique, it cost the son a chance at getting the job.

The Boomer Trap

There is a major danger or trap associated with targeting the Baby Boomer generation. A Baby Boomer born in 1946 had very different life experiences than someone who has a birthday in the 1962 calendar year. Yet, traditionally, both would be considered Baby Boomers. Someone born in 1946 was 16 years old in the 1962. That was within about a year of the John F. Kennedy assassination in November of 1963. They were about 23 when Neil Armstrong walked on the moon and 28 in 1974 when Nixon resigned. Their generation was defined in large part by the 1960s civil rights movement, the Vietnam War and the walk on the moon.

A Baby Boomer born in 1962 was about 1 year old when Kennedy was assassinated, around 7 when Neil Armstrong walked on the moon and approximately 12 when Nixon resigned from the White House. A Baby Boomer born in 1962 experienced the energy crisis and the disco craze that was embodied in the 1977 classic movie "Saturday Night Fever." My wife, Christine, was born in the early 1960s and "Saturday Night Fever" is her all-time favorite movie. The Iranian hostage crisis of 1979 happened when these 1962 Baby Boomers were 17 years old. Ronald Reagan was elected president in 1980 when many of them turned 18. The bottom line is that a birth span of almost 20 years is too large to define the Baby Boomer generation as one group of people. People born in the 1940s grew up with Elvis, Bobby Darin, The Beatles, James Brown, The Rolling Stones, Chuck Berry, The Four Tops, The Doors, Jimi Hendrix, Eric Burdon and the Animals, "I Love Lucy," "Howdy Doody," "Andy Griffith" and "The Dick Van Dyke Show."

So called Baby Boomers born in the early '60s are much more likely to identify with "M*A*S*H," "The Brady Bunch" "All in the Family," "Good Times," "Welcome Back Kotter," "The Jeffersons," Lynyrd Skynyrd, Boston, John Travolta, Sly and the Family Stone, Journey, Kool and the Gang and .38 Special. The Baby Boomer trap is to lump both of these groups together. The Practical Growth Leaders and marketers that win consistently with Boomers will learn how to break these differences into separate and distinctive generations as well as market segments. What motivates early Boomers versus late Boomers can be very different depending on the product category.

Generation Jones

There is a growing recognition of the vast age difference between those born in the first part vs. the latter part of the big post-WWII baby boom. Those differences are so great that these segments are increasingly being viewed as two separate generations. The most effective and widely recognized segmentation is entitled Generation Jones, as defined by Jonathan Pontell, a well known social commentator and generations expert. He defines Generation Jones as the group of people born between 1954-1965. This group was always told they were Baby Boomers, but they didn't really identify with their Baby Boomer counterparts. In a recent interview I conducted with Pontell, he shared the distinctive characteristics of the Generation Jones group born between 1954 and 1965. Here are some of the key facts Pontell shared with me regarding this powerful generation:

- Generation Jones represents 26 percent of all adults in the U.S. that are 18 years old and older. This is versus 16 percent of all 18+ adults in the U.S. that are true Baby Boomers born prior to 1954. In addition, most generational experts now also accept that the true Baby Boom actually started in 1942-43 prior to the end of World War II.

- Generation Jones represents 42 percent of all adults making over $100,000 a year. Approximately 47 percent of all adults that install a pool or spa are Jonesers.

• Generation Jones spends more dollars on-line than any other generation. Approximately 41 percent of all consumers who spent $2,500 or more on the internet were Jonesers. True Baby Boomers have been slower on average to adapt to the internet or try new leading edge technology.

Pontell indicated that there is a rational consciousness awakening that defining Baby Boomers as one single group is a very costly mistake, particularly in light of the huge opportunity that Generation Jones represents. Not only is GenJones the largest and highest-income-earning U.S. generation, but there is also considerable research revealing that Jonesers are now very persuadable vis-à-vis marketing messaging. This insight has been a surprising discovery to many marketers, given that conventional wisdom typically assigns this high level of reachability to younger consumers. The unique ongoing generational personality of Jonesers combines with their current point in the life cycle to create a powerful opportunity for marketers. Jonesers are currently taking stock of their lives, leaving them much more experimental and open to trying new ideas, products, and services than forty-somethings traditionally are. Marketers including global advertising agencies and major brands are now focusing on the unique characteristics of Generation Jones in their creative and marketing planning. Marketers that are ahead of the curve with this fifth generation will own a unique, distinctive and powerful position in the marketplace. This largest, most affluent and highly-persuadable generation represents the largest, single-generational marketing opportunity available to leverage incremental business growth.

BOOMj.com

A number of Baby Boomer websites have been introduced in recent years. One of the major players in this venue is BOOMj.com. It is a comprehensive one-stop 360 degree network that clearly understands the distinction between Baby Boomers and Generation Jonesers. In fact, the letter "j" in its brand name directly refers to Generation Jones and the importance it represents. BOOMj.com is an all inclusive social and lifestyle network specifically designed for Baby Boomers and Generation Jones. BOOMj is the complete one-stop network for Baby Boomers and Jonesers. It combines a social network to connect with new friends and share your life experiences. It enables you to learn more about your interests with others by offering a travel service to find the best value get-aways. There is also a BOOMj virtual store that sells over 1 million items targeted to these two powerful generations. The full BOOMj experience includes late breaking news in health, finance and lifestyle sections that are specifically targeted to Baby Boomers and Generation Jonesers. BOOMj represents a powerful integrated and inclusive social network that combines a strong emotional connection with a strong functional value. The fully integrated one-stop site for Baby Boomers and Generation Jones represents a powerful platform to communicate, influence, inspire and motivate these two critical generations.

Generational Segmentation Caution

It is important to also approach the Generation X (born 1965-1977) and Millennial Generation (born 1978-2000) with the same degree of caution. Much like the earlier Boomer example, life experiences for someone born in 1980 versus 1990 are also different as it relates to the Millennial Generation. The same could be said for a Gen-Xer born in 1967 versus 1977. It is important to emphasize that while the five generations and their differences are real, the need to further segment within both Generation X and Millennials is also very important. It is also important to understand that these generations can vary significantly on a global scale. This is particularly the case in developed vs. undeveloped countries. A recent seminar participant at a global company told me that television was not even available in his country until 1975. This certainly leads to a different timeline for generational attitude development in his country vs. the United States, the United Kingdom, Western Europe and Japan. Generational segmentation will continue to evolve in the coming years as Practical Growth Leaders work hard to discover more original insights about the unique perspectives and marketplace behaviors of these groups.

Women Case Study

At Hallmark, I spent nearly half my life marketing to women and I loved every minute of it! I would estimate that approximately 90 percent of the greeting cards sent in the United States are purchased by women. The only exception is Valentine's Day where I would venture it falls all the way down to 80 percent women. However, if you go into any store on Valentine's Day, February 14, you will see 98 percent men ... desperate men! Greeting cards have always been a category dominated by women. It has always been a category that has been all but ignored by men – with that one-day exception.

The marketplace landscape is changing faster than ever before. Remember the Apple Super Bowl ad called "1984" that aired January 22, 1984 and introduced the Apple Macintosh personal computer in the United States? A female heroine ran past the security guards to the workers' assembly. She was carrying a sledge hammer, which she launched at a giant screen that featured a video of "Big

Brother." The screen exploded and a powerful voice proclaimed, "On January 24, 1984, Apple Computer will introduce Macintosh and you'll see why 1984 won't be like 1984!" "Advertising Age" named the spot the "Commercial of the Decade." A 1999 copy of "TV Guide" called it one of the "Top 50 Commercials of All Time." The spot is one of the most memorable ads I have ever seen.

We need to book that same female heroine again, to launch a new sledge hammer announcing the new age of marketing in diverse ways to women.

Growing Female Influence

As noted earlier, the growing influence of women in the marketplace will make this market segment much more powerful in the coming years. Women conservatively make at least 70 percent plus of all the purchasing decisions. A recent "Business Week" article refers to women as almost every family's "Chief Purchasing Officer." The stunning development proves women are now the major decision-makers in the more traditionally male dominated areas of home improvement and electronics. New laptops are being introduced in green, powder blue and pink and weigh in at a very light four pounds. Computer all purpose bags are now specifically targeted toward women. Apple has introduced several small I-Pods in multiple styles and colors focused on the female market. Women value editorial and hard information much more than hard hitting advertising. Endorsements from celebrity influencers like "Oprah" and "Ellen," along with editorials in magazines women trust are absolutely critical to future purchase decisions.

Consider that one out of every five homes is purchased by a single woman. Also, consider that approximately 50 percent of all women live alone. There are many social and economic trends that have contributed to these numbers. In the end, the only detail that really matters to the Practical Growth Leader is that the number of women living alone is expected to continue to grow.

What are the priorities of single women? What is on their mind? Clearly, they are concerned about financial security, health, wellness, creating social connections, owning and caring for a home, growing their independence and living life to the fullest. So, what does all this mean for the following industries?

- Hardware stores
- Financial advisors
- Mortgage providers and realtors
- Automobile industry
- Travel industry

Hardware Stores

Hardware retailers who design stores with wide aisles, appropriate lighting, bright colors and superior customer service will win this growing market segment because more women are shopping in hardware stores. More single Baby Boomer women are buying homes in established neighborhoods every day. These homes are a major reflection on the women who buy them and represent a strong emotional connection. They represent success, nesting, security, nostalgia and independence. The homeowners will want to engage in their own home improvement projects and need help to do it. They are increasingly showing up in hardware stores. Women will want a more detailed process description of the steps involved in a home improvement project. In *The Female Mind,* Dr. Louann Brizendine writes that the average woman says 20,000 words a day, compared to 7,000 for the average man. The bottom line is women will tend to ask more questions than men. The hardware retailer who understands this and develops a customer interaction plan around it will earn sustainable loyalty from this growing market segment. Westlake ACE Hardware is a successful and growing Midwest chain that is highly committed to customer service. While I was teaching an advertising course at Baker University in Kansas City, one of the single, female students mentioned that Westlake ACE Hardware was her favorite store. When I asked her why, she said it was because of her "Westlake guy." She said that she recently purchased a home in an established neighborhood and often went to her Westlake ACE Hardware store for help. Her "Westlake guy" always went out of his way to help her and answer all of her questions. Even more importantly, he always told her that if she had any problems with the project when she got home, she could always call him or come back to the store and they would solve it together. What a great story about customer service. I recently had the honor of attending the Westlake ACE Hardware Management Conference Awards Banquet. I was speaking to their store management team the next day. Peer recognition tied to specific sales and financial results made this event a combination of a high energy business celebration, rock concert and sporting event. After attending their celebration and meeting, I can easily understand why they have a passion for customer service. Westlake ACE is a powerful culture that has a clear focus on achieving results and having fun along the way!

Women vs. Men Shopping Behavior

Compare that scenario to my own personal perspective. I look like a typical hardware guy, but really don't have a clue when it comes to a do-it yourself project. However, I would never let anyone know that when I walk into a hardware store. In fact, I usually say "no" when someone asks if I need any help. (By the way, I never like to ask for directions on family vacations either.)

The difference between women and men can be illustrated in how they shop for Valentine's Day cards. Women take their time to read several different cards, taking them out of the card rack and putting each one back until they find just the right one that comes from the heart. Too many men, on the other hand, tend to look for the wife caption on the cover, glance at the words inside a card and then bolt for the cash register! February 14th is a great day to experience the many differences in the emotional connections between women and men. Women tend to view communication as a continuous process, while men view it as a series of separate events. This is important for a man to remember when he reports to a woman. She will ask, on average, more questions than a male boss. This does not mean she does not trust what the man is telling her. She is simply asking questions as part of the process of communication.

Financial Advisors

Consider that Baby Boomers control almost 70 percent of the wealth in the United States and "USA Today" recently reported that women still outlive men by an average of five years. The good news for men is that the gap used to be eight years. Guys are becoming more health conscious, exercising more and smoking less. That said, women still hold a significant edge in average life span. You don't have to be a financial rocket scientist to figure out that Baby Boomer women are going to be making the largest number of financial advisor choices to manage the future wealth. Add fuel to the fire with over 50 percent of all women living alone, and a clear picture of the next decade emerges. Financial advisors will need to tailor a substantial portion of their marketing and selling efforts directly toward single women. This will be an incredible growth area for financial advisors in the coming years. Those companies that distinguish themselves and emotionally connect with the financial needs women have will achieve breakthrough market share growth. Practical Growth Leaders will navigate the rapids of change and focus more resources on the marketing potential of women. The elevation of women as decision-makers across all industries will have a profound impact on virtually every business moving forward.

Mortgage Providers and Realtors

Consider how the growing influence of single women will impact the mortgage provider and real estate business. Mortgage companies that cater specifically to women will make more loans and grow market share. The companies that have mortgage plans specifically designed to satisfy the special needs of single women will win in the marketplace. Realtors who understand how to find the right financial solutions for single women combined with appropriate community lifestyles such as social connections, good security, clubhouse pools, maintenance free and fewer kids next door will build their sales with this growing market. The move by single women into established neighborhoods also represents a significant market opportunity for mortgage loan providers and realtors to leverage to effectively grow their business. This trend will continue for several more years. It will not only be about responding to these special needs, but also how you effectively merchandise the specific services you offer to this growing market segment that will ultimately make the difference.

Automobile Industry

Can you think of any process in the history of the world that is more confusing, intimidating, frustrating and gut wrenching than going to an automobile dealership and negotiating for a new or used car? I remember an incident at a dealership where I was considering buying a car about five years ago. There I was in the salesman's office going over the deal and making another round of intense counter offers. My salesperson left to see the manager and I noticed right across from me in another office was a woman in a similar meeting with another salesman. Suddenly, she exploded and said, "You are trying to take advantage of me because I am a woman!" More senior salespeople and the sales manager swarmed to the office, saying that they would never take advantage of her. They left, saying they would further review her counter offer. After the swarm left her alone in the office, we were separated only by two glass windows. She looked at me, smiled confidently and turned away. Who do you think got the better deal that day? I will always believe that she did! Unfortunately, this story illustrates why the automobile industry has had a poor perceived track record regarding its sensitivity to the female market. This makes no sense when you consider how women directly or indirectly influence car purchases.

Practical Growth Leaders who crack the code on selling cars in a high-integrity fashion to single women will win major-share gains in the coming years. They will position themselves as a destination spot for this growing market segment, with special services oriented toward women. According to Marti Barletta at "BrandWeek", 60 percent of all cars are purchased by women and they play a key role in influencing almost 85 percent of the end purchases. Women will view shopping as a longer process with many more questions around safety, fuel efficiency and style design. Companies that satisfy this need with a shopping process, environment and negotiation dynamics for the female customer stand to win her mind, heart and business.

Travel Industry

The fact is more and more women are taking vacations alone. Fifty percent of the women in the United States are living alone and this has created a growing and influential market for cruise lines, all-inclusive resorts, hotels and a variety of travel services. Single women are finding that there are some key benefits to traveling alone such as no competing agendas, more schedule flexibility and a lack of pressure of involving others' needs on the trips.

The Practical Growth Leader who understands how to package travel experiences for women traveling alone will experience growth in market share. Packages tailored specifically to women vacationing alone should include opportunities to connect with others traveling by themselves, arrangements available for dining out, maximum itinerary flexibility and several sight seeing options that would be comfortable to pursue at one's leisure. Security and safety would also be important for anyone vacationing alone. The travel companies who understand, embrace, and tailor their offering specifically to women will win a substantial growth in business and long-term loyalty from this growing and influential market segment.

It is important to note that more and more married women are taking extended trips, alone and together, without their husbands. Women traveling together create a strong bond of companionship and are a growing and influential market segment. Travel services that schedule group activities for women will build their business in a sustainable way over time. Married women are increasingly taking trips with other women to strengthen friendships with each other. At the same time, their male counterparts are increasingly doing more things with their kids. For example, a good friend of mine has been vacationing for many years with his son, as they continue their journey to visit every Major League Baseball stadium in North America. These trips can create special memories that last a lifetime.

Innovation-Chasing Growth Segments

It is hard to imagine that the influence on the economy, shopping patterns, financial markets, health issues and our society as a whole for the next 20 years will be impacted more by any two generations than Baby Boomers and Generation Jones. It is also hard to over-estimate the growing impact and influence of women on the marketplace and how this trend will impact future purchase decisions. These cases illustrate the need to invest your innovation resources against Gold Growth Segments. Think about it. Would you rather invest your resources where you have declining, mature or growth curves? The answer is not complicated.

Find the growth corridors outlined earlier adjacent to your core business and identify your PAC Power. Determine where you have permission to go and the capabilities to deliver the products or services. Then, overlay your PAC Power against Gold Growth Segments that matter both short-term and long-term. Determine the relative and potential size of these growth segments. Focus your innovations and capabilities against these segments that are growing in marketplace influence. Many companies make the mistake of incrementally innovating against shrinking market segments. While this may deliver some impressive short-term gains, it rarely results in sustainable long-term growth. It is also critical that when leveraging your PAC Power with innovation, you do so throughout the value chain. Moving to the growth side of the curve is about more than product innovation. It is being innovative around everything you do. Most companies have a definition of innovation that is product focused and too narrow. The fact is all employees have an innovator living inside them. Your job as a Practical Growth Leader is to find the innovator living inside each of your people and bring it to the surface. Who knows? You may have another Betty Nesmith, who invented "White Out," working on your team right now.

Avoiding Innovation Sand Traps

Practical Growth Leaders always need to be aware of the sand traps associated with innovation. As golfers are well aware, sand traps are hazards to stay away from as you navigate a course. I know a great deal about sand traps. I spend most of my time in them when I am trying to play golf. The following sand traps need to be avoided as you focus on innovative solutions.

1. Don't take your focus off the core business. If you reallocate the majority of your resources toward innovation, the core business could decline

rapidly. Since most companies fund their innovation initiatives from core business profits, beware of what can happen when the cash cow becomes restless. If the core business rapidly deteriorates due to the stripping of resources that are redirected toward new initiatives, testing and future growth, your ability to innovate may evaporate right along with your bottom line. How many times have you heard business executives say we are going back to our core business?

2. Avoid falling in love with innovation initiatives. It is critical that the leaders and the teams working on these initiatives have passion and believe with their hearts in what they are doing every day. However, the Practical Growth Leader must look at each of these initiatives from a ruthless and objective standpoint.

3. If it's not working, adjust or pull the plug quickly. Many times I have seen leaders believe that if they just stay the course a little longer, sales from an innovation initiative will turn around. It almost never happens.

4. Capture the learning from innovation initiatives. No one in any company wants to greet a new, innovative idea with "we tried that before and it was a disaster." However, there is a need to capture the learning over time and share it throughout your company to learn from the mistakes of the past. The idea of centralizing this learning in one place to serve as a company resource is a great way to bring objectivity to this captured learning.

5. Be careful how much you credit or how much you publicly praise leadership that works on innovation vs. your team members that pull the heavy load of the core business every day. If you are continually and publicly enamored only with the accomplishments of your innovation teams, your best leaders that focus only on the core business are likely to leave your organization. Your core profits may leave right along with them.

6. Innovate within the core business! How should the core business be reinvented throughout your value chain? The biggest ideas are often the most simple and are usually right in front of us.

Summary

The Practical Growth Leader who innovates successfully and consistently will almost always wind up in the winner's circle. John Kennedy once said, "Why play for second place when first is available?" I would add this notion: "Why settle for being a follower on innovation when you can win the race?" Think of our great moments in history. Major events such as the first man on the moon in 1969 were created because of the combination of permission, imagination, influence and capabilities. As he climbed down the lunar module's ladder to become the first man to step on the moon's surface, Neil Armstrong proclaimed, "One small step for man, one giant leap for mankind." Practical Growth Leaders know that leading innovation is not a small step for the faint of heart. You must combine the large steps of permission, influence and capabilities with a competitive desire to win every day in the marketplace.

What's Next?

I love competition! It is the life blood that makes us better every day. Competition keeps us sharp and focused to win. Are you ready to go on a journey to find the Fast Passing Zones that enable you to move past your competitors to a first-place finish? I am reminded of a few lines from "Radar Love," a classic from a group called Golden Earring. "No more speed, I'm almost there. Gotta keep cool now, gotta take care. Last car to pass, here I go. And the line of cars drove down real slow . . ."

Buckle up and get ready because we are about to kick it in high gear and go after the Fast Passing Zones!

Are you ready to take the Step 4 hurdle test?

Step 4 Hurdle Test

1. What is P A C Power?
2. What are the five components to a "fast break" innovation culture?
3. Who is Generation Jones? How do they compare to Baby Boomers?
4. How will the growing influence in the purchasing power of women impact your business? (If at all)
5. What are the six key innovation sand traps that every Practical Growth Leader should consider in their planning process?

90-Day Innovation Flex Plan

Time Frame	Activities
30 Days	Where are the PAC Power opportunities in your business? What are the top three you and your team could leverage? What three to five specific culture changes will you and your team make to drive innovation within your organization?
60 Days	What are the top two Gold Growth Segment opportunities that fit within growth corridor intersections adjacent to your core business? Are you currently chasing growth, mature, or declining segments with your resources? What specific innovation sand traps do you have in your organization that will need to be avoided by Practical Growth Leaders?
90 Days	Assess the "niche" growth core corridor opportunities from a resource perspective. Do you need additional resources to chase the opportunities? What additional internal resources or outside strategic partnerships are needed to deliver your PAC Power initiatives to the marketplace?

CHAPTER 5

Step 5: Find the Passing Zones to Finish First

Competitive Attitude

When I think of competition, I am reminded of what the "Whopper" computer said to Professor Stephen Falken in the 1983 classic movie "War Games."

"Greetings Professor Falken, how about a nice game of chess?" The key to moving ahead of your competition, and staying there, is how many moves you think ahead. It is the difference between a relaxing game of checkers and the classic strategy game of chess. While playing checkers, you basically read and react to the game as it develops in front of you. Chess requires a much higher level of focus on your strategy and the potential future moves of your competitor. Former Pro Football Hall of Fame running back, Marcus Allen, once said, "I never worry about the tackler in front of me, I'm looking two to three moves down the field – like I'm playing chess. You have to think ahead, or you don't survive for long in the NFL." That is true in any competitive business. To succeed, you must accept contingency planning and account for multiple scenarios.

I remember riding in a Procter & Gamble Company car in St. Louis with a Division Sales Manager about 30 years ago when the topic of competition surfaced in the conversation. He mentioned that most companies "underestimate their competitors" and fail to spend enough time considering the potential moves they will make that directly impact their business. The other piece of advice in that conversation was to "expect to fail, but be prepared to succeed."

The more I thought about this comment, the more I realized it was a message about the preparation, passion and tenacity needed to beat the competition every day. If you let up or take a day, a week, or a quarter lightly, you will lose. Think about it. Compare leaders' comments we often hear in meetings today. It is fashionable today to say, "We have no competition; our only real competitor is ourselves." Another often used quote is, "We really don't believe our competitors are in the same business we are in with our customers."

Still another is, "We focus on innovation rather than the competition." Most of these comments are driven by ignorance, arrogance and/or insecurity. The fact is that regardless of your business, Practical Growth Leaders know your competition is trying to beat your brains out every day. We built the 8 Cs of the Practical Growth Leader concept in Step 1. It was about caring and emotionally connecting with your people. This step involves running with the Seven Rs when dealing with your competition. They are: Ruthless, Relentless, Respectful, Resourceful, Resilient, Responsive and Results oriented. The competition game must always be played within the chalk-lines of business integrity and ethics. This chapter is about going to war with your competition and winning every day. As Bruce Springsteen sang in "Born To Run," a classic that served as an anthem for an entire generation in the late 1970s and 1980s, "We're fuel injected... steppin' out over the line!" During my business career, I always got out of bed every morning motivated, in part, by a deep personal hatred of the competition. I don't hate the individuals personally. I do, however, detest the organizations they work for. I am not kidding. In fact, I believed that when a customer purchased a product or service from one of my competitors, they were taking money directly out of my kids' college fund. This may sound too radical or personal to you. I am speaking from my heart and I believe it is true. One connection point people often fail to make is how competitive actions can directly impact their personal as well as professional lives. If your competitors succeed against your leadership and company, jobs will be eliminated, salaries, as well as bonuses negatively impacted, and it will be a lot less fun to come to work every day with the feeling of losing in the marketplace. Does that sound personal enough to you? The fact is there are other people and companies out there who want to take your customers away as well as your and your family's standard of living. If you have ever been a victim of downsizing, chances are a competitor may have played a significant role in contributing to your situation.

Fast Passing Zone Concept

Now that we have established the importance of your competitors on a professional and personal level, it is time to focus on how to win the game. The following model highlights how to leverage your strengths against your competitors' weaknesses to build your business. The model focuses on competitive points of leverage where your competitors are weak in areas that are critical to your current and potential customers. You must locate and leverage these passing zones to move into the first place position. When you combine

PAC Power (customer Permission And Capabilities) against competitive weaknesses defined as critical by your largest customers, you can focus your resources with leverage to create a Fast Passing Zone. The following diagram illustrates the competitive Fast Passing Zone concept:

Concept 5.1

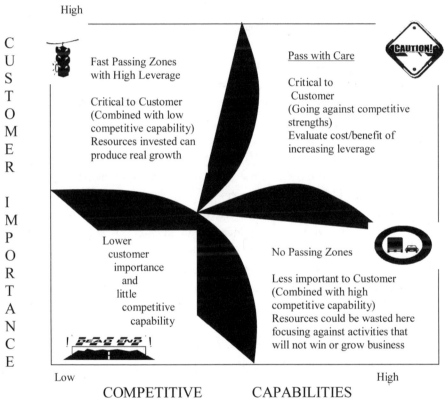

Fast Passing Zone Concept

The first step is to find the Fast Passing Zones where you can gain leverage over your competitor by better satisfying a need that is critical to the customer. These are the weak links of your competition that are top of mind for your potential and future clients/customers. The Pass With Care Zone is worth exploring to determine more effective solutions you can bring to the customers' table. This will put pressure on your competition. Keep in mind that this is a competitive capability strength zone that may have higher barriers to investment.

Finally, where client/customer assessment of deliverables is lower in priority, and where competitive capabilities are high represents a No Passing Zone that would require high investment and result in very little incremental client/customer growth.

How Do You Build Your Fast Passing Zone Concept?

Your Fast Passing Zone Concept begins with the Peacetime Customer Interviews reviewed in Step 3, regarding customer loyalty. Interview your clients/customers about your strengths and weaknesses as well as your key competitors. Conduct the interview as a separate meeting. Don't try to sell them something. This is what we mean by peacetime. Openly ask them to rank the key characteristics of the key deliverables of your business. Then ask them how you are performing against those key variables versus your competition. It is critical to also directly ask your customers how your competitors are performing along the same dimensions. I would highly recommend you consider having a third party do the interview on your behalf. That will allow your clients and customers to open up more and be very candid without allowing relationships to get in the way. Don't try to do surgery on yourself. A great surgeon would not attempt to remove his own appendix. This feedback will be far more objective and useful. This unfiltered process will give you an advantage over any competitor. It will also allow you to build into interviews questions that customers deem important and rank high in their deliverables. Examples include the need for the following key customer deliverables, which also represent potential competitive vulnerabilities:

- There is a need for more custom tailoring
- Lack of innovation in key areas
- Level of customer service unacceptable or below expectations and why
- Industry knowledge about marketplace developments
- Ability to decide and execute quickly is lacking
- Poor past performance in categories important to the customer
- Lack of strong top-to-top relationships
- Lack of follow-through and trust issues

Identify the soft vulnerable area of your competitors and exploit it to your full potential. In football, this is known as "taking what the defense gives you." Why do most football coaches script the first 15 to 20 offensive plays of a game? They want to probe an opposing defense to see how they will react in certain situations as the game progresses. These interviews allow you to ask probing questions without your competitors participating in the process.

How to Apply the Fast Passing Zone

Utilizing the customer competitive dimensions, let's work through one example of how we can exploit a Fast Passing Zone. Assume we have just interviewed a customer where we share the business with two other competitors. We just learned in our Peacetime Customer Interview that our customers believe the competition is coming up short in response to their specific innovation needs. We discover that the customer believes this is a critical aspect to growing their future business. The customer has communicated this to our competitors several times. Despite the best efforts of our competitors, the customer still perceives their response is less than stellar. The same customer has told us we are stronger in this area of innovation than either one of our two competitors. Now is the time to scramble all of our resources and attack the competition. We have just identified a Fast Passing Zone where we have the advantage, capability and leverage to deliver innovative solutions at a much higher level than our competitors. We can use this as leverage with this customer to gain more business. In this example, doing the innovation initiative to outflank your competitors is only step one. Step two is to aggressively merchandise your innovation progress on an ongoing basis with your customer. Periodically review your innovation progress at least once a quarter (or more often if appropriate). Refer to these merchandising sessions that are focused on innovation when asking for more business. The point is if you don't ask for it, you won't win. Customers and clients don't want to change their business relationships. It is a hard thing to do. Remember, the biggest decisions in life are emotional. It leads to tough and hard decisions to make phone calls followed up usually by an intense meeting to try to contest or change the customer's decision. If you move into enough Fast Passing Zones with a given client or customer, you have given them all the information they need to make a thoughtful decision on a brand, a company, a store, a product or service. When it all comes together, I am reminded of the song title of the 1980 Queen classic, "Another One Bites The Dust." Your competitor is now very close to being left in your dust, wondering what went wrong.

Five Competitive Rules of the Road

There are five Rules of the Road to keep in mind relative to your competitors:

1. Don't ever underestimate what competitors do to your company and clients/customers. The corporate world is littered with companies that were casualties of focused and powerful competitors.

2. Do you understand who your competitors really are in the broadest sense? Many companies and industries have failed to wake up and discover that their product category or brand has lost relevance and value. Are you in the CD business competing against other suppliers of compact discs or are you in the music business competing against I-tunes, I-Pods, etc.? The answer is, of course, both. Yes, you are competing within a given format for music business. However, you are also in the music choice business competing with every other format outside of compact discs as well. The Practical Growth Leader knows you must define your business both narrowly and broadly to make sure you have the appropriate short-term and long-term field of vision.

3. A great way to test the strength of one of your own ideas is to stop and think: How would I feel or react if my competitor started doing this tomorrow morning? If the answer is it would make you feel awful, you probably have a great idea on your hands to drive business.

4. Monitor competitive changes in the marketplace with key and trusted customers providing you with immediate feedback. It is critical that you have a strong relationship with key customers who are comfortable sharing competitive information with you in a timely way.

5. Never directly talk to a competitor about your business. It can compromise everything. Discussions about the weather, traffic, sports, vacations and lifestyles are fine. There are also many industry associations where competitors meet and work together for the "good of the industry." As Sergeant Phil Esterhaus (played by Michael Conrad) of "Hill Street Blues" told his officers each morning, "Hey, hey... let's be careful out there!" Anytime you are in a room with a competitor, never forget the dynamics of your relationship. As long as a competitor is willing to talk about their business, just smile, listen, learn and say nothing.

Running with the Seven Rs

To consistently beat the competition, you must run your business with the Seven Rs when dealing with your business rivals. The Seven Rs represent the following leadership behaviors:

- Ruthless
- Relentless
- Respectful
- Resourceful
- Resilient
- Responsive
- Results focused

Tony Soprano (played by Emmy winner James Gandolfini), the star of the classic HBO series, "The Sopranos," said, "You're supposed to be earners. That's why you have the top positions." It is important to remember that your competitors want to take your personal capability "to earn" a market leadership position away.

1. Ruthless

Your competitors want to diminish your company and your own personal standard of living. When you get the competition in a vulnerable position, you must be ruthless in your focus to drive your business. This may sound extreme or draconian, but it is true. In the 1970 movie, "Patton," Oscar winner George C. Scott said in a memorable scene, "I don't like to pay for the same real estate twice." From my perspective, what that means is once you have your competitor on the run, put the pedal to the metal and never let up. If you let up when things are going well, you will wind up paying for the same real estate twice. While ruthless is a good description of how you should focus on your competition, it is also important to remember that the game must always be played with the highest ethics, morals and standards. I cannot begin to tell you how many times in my business career I let my opponents up off the mat. As a result, I wound up "paying for the same real estate twice."

2. Relentless

Forrest Gump, played by Academy Award winner Tom Hanks, uttered the famous line: "Mama always said life is like a box of chocolates, you never know what you're gonna get." The same thing could be said about your competition. You never know what surprises they will come up with. Great companies win because they stay focused and out-hustle the competition. They convert market data into insights that can be translated quickly into tangible value in the marketplace. The same principle could be applied to how you approach your business with the competition. Customers will give you a lot of credit for being first to the marketplace. If you can find the Fast Passing Zones and then focus your resources on those areas, you can leave your competitors in the dust. The truth is most companies are not relentless in their focus. Many companies change strategies every 12 to 18 months and hire a steady stream of consultants to justify their changes in strategic direction.

Part of being relentless in your focus to beat our competition and finish first is to merchandise and promote everything you do with your customers to get full credit and ultimately to change their behavior. Late and great Baseball Hall of Famer Bill Veeck, a maverick owner who dreamed up outlandish promotions, was famous for his creativity. People would stream into his park just to see what Veeck was offering that game. He once said, "When you don't promote, a terrible thing happens... nothing." Failure to effectively merchandise and promote your work to customers leads to the downfall of many powerful brands and companies. You must be relentless throughout the value chain including how you merchandise and communicate success stories to your customers. Many companies and leaders are self-effacing and don't like to brag. The bottom line is simple, if you don't take credit for being first with your customers, your competitors will be happy to assume the pace car position.

3. Respectful

What do we mean by being respectful of your competition? It goes far beyond not underestimating your competitor. It involves walking in your competitors' shoes. Companies that do this effectively often ask a small team of people to pretend they are the competition and develop game scenarios around what a competitor is likely to do to strategically respond to marketplace changes or major initiatives your company may or may not launch. These war games exercises take your competitive awareness to a whole new level. It also facilitates a simulated game of chess where you can develop game scenario moves and counter moves versus your competitors. Most companies do not create these small teams to behave as your major competitors. If you do it, and do it effectively, your increased competitive awareness will be likely to yield big dividends. You will also gain credibility if this is included in any business recommendation you take forward or implement.

4. Resourceful

Are you able to pull together the right resources in critical mass to exploit your competitors' weaknesses to drive your business? There are many leaders who are aware of the weaknesses of their competitors. These leaders would exploit them to their advantage, but are unable to muster the right resources at the right place, at the right time, to do it. When faced with this challenge, my first question deals with the leadership of the company. Is there a common view of reality, zeroing in on the greatest opportunities to grow the business? My experience is that most of the time the resources are available, they are simply allocated to support a different area of the business. The effective Practical Growth Leader must be able to deliver a compelling case to obtain the funding and other resources needed. They can expect to be financially challenged for the return on investment business case. To quote Academy Award winner Cuba Gooding's line from "Jerry Maguire," the popular Tom Cruise movie, "Show me the money!"

Another critical part of being resourceful is to be creative about how you will reallocate resources and come up with new solutions to move into the Fast Passing Zones. There will be many times that you do not have the resources to effectively compete, but part of the job of a Practical Growth Leader is to find a creative way to do it anyway. A large number of practical growth plans have been built and delivered superior results armed only with bailing wire, duct tape and other non-incremental resources.

5. Resilient

Can you and your company take a knock down punch from a competitor that really negatively impacts your business? Can you absorb the shock to your company's central nervous system and still keep the teams focused with a "steady as she goes" philosophy? This is the toughest part of going up against quality competitors every day. Some days you are going to lose. Most leaders don't want to admit it or accept that true statement. The true measure of any Practical Growth Leader is how they rally the troops after a major loss. It is easy to be a growth leader when you are winning. It goes back to that classic Right Guard deodorant commercial: "Never let them see you sweat." You should look for ways to interject lightness and humor after a big loss. I am reminded of how I would call a special meeting with my team immediately following a big loss. We would sit down and learn our painful lessons together. The more important reason for the meeting, though, was to put the loss behind us and move on to focus on those things we can control. We had just lost a key piece of business to a competitor. The team was at an all-time low point and that is where true leadership must emerge to turn things around.

Focus on the key lessons from the loss and quickly reset the table for winning the next piece of business available. Motivate your team to look only forward and not to dwell on a painful loss. This is the most difficult aspect of being a Practical Growth Leader. The best Practical Growth Leaders are consistent and resilient. They actually become more outwardly calm as the storm clouds threaten.

6. Responsive

How do you respond to a change in your competitors' strategy? What processes do you have in place to learn about the change within hours after it is introduced into the marketplace to your customers? A slow response time to competitive changes in the marketplace is called a sustainable competitive disadvantage. Does this mean you should quickly respond to everything your competitor changes in the marketplace to your customers? Absolutely not. It means you must learn about the change within the first few hours of introduction, quickly have the right people in place to assess its implications, develop the pros and cons to various alternative responses and execute the decision. The right decision might be to stay the course and do nothing differently. The key to being responsive is simple. Learn about the competitive change. Evaluate the pros vs. cons of various alternatives and respond to the marketplace with any adjustments that are needed to win.

7. Results Focused

A national sales manager at Procter & Gamble once told me that "only results count." The best part of Running with the 7 Rs of competition is that in the end, only results count. The results concept of finishing first is critical because it forces us to agree how we are all being measured. Are we growing or declining in sales, market share and profitability? How can you align common measures with how your customer is evaluated? Where are the biggest future opportunities to take business away from our competitors? The competitive spinning wheel concept below highlights how Running With the 7 Rs behaviors revolve around the Fast Passing Zones to finish first!

Concept 5.2

7 Rs Competitive Leadership Behavior Wheel Concept

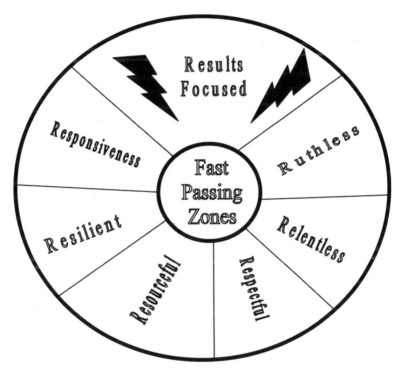

Unlike the game show "The Wheel of Fortune," where contestants can win cash depending on where the wheel stops, the leadership behavior wheel of Fast Passing Zones is controlled by you and your team. This translates into bad news for your competitors.

Summary

In order to beat the competition, you must first hate to lose. You must take what your competition is trying to do to you and your lifestyle every day very personally. In the classic movie, "Apocalypse Now," Captain Kilgore (played by

Robert Duvall) proudly proclaimed, "I love the smell of Napalm in the morning. It smells like victory." That phrase has been used in several hundred recent pop culture references, television shows and paraphrased in countless other movies. I would say that I love the sight of any competitor struggling in the morning. The war with the competition will never end, and starts over every single day with the rising sun.

Step 5 focused on how to go about utilizing the Fast Passing Zones concept to finish first. It also covered the five rules of the road to observe when dealing with competitors. Finally, we highlighted Running with the 7 Rs behaviors to use to defeat your competition and grow your business. The key step change is to align your customer measures by determining what really matters in the buying decision. Identify where your competitors are weak on these critical dimensions and leverage your capabilities directly against them to win more business. The key is to stay focused and play offense.

What's Next?

In his classic, "On the Road Again," Willie Nelson sang: "I'm going places that I've never been." Are you ready to clear the hurdle of Step 5? Are you ready to move on toward Step 6 where we will successfully Build the Growth Curves? Are you ready to go places you have never been? It starts with building growth in the core business. Do you know where your business stands on the growth curve? Stay tuned! We are about to find out.

Step 5 Hurdle Test

1. Can you define the key elements of the Fast Passing Zone concept?
2. What tools can you use to build your specific business Fast Passing Zone model?
3. What are the five rules of the road to keep in mind when you engage the competition?
4. What are the 7 Rs (behaviors) you can run with to win in the Fast Passing Zones?
5. What does being "respectful" to a competitor and their capabilities mean to your business?

90-Day "Passing Zones" Flex Plan

Time Frame	Activities

30 Days	Begin your Peacetime Customer Interviews to assess:
	  – What matters
	  – Where competition is weak
	  – Where competition is strong
	  – Where your company is strong vs. weaknesses
	Develop your own Fast Passing Zone concept applicable only to your specific business

60 Days	Find the Fast Passing Zones for your business where:
	  – It is critical to the customer
	  – It is currently a competitive weakness
	  – You own a key strength to deliver what matters at a consistently superior level
	
	What incremental or reallocated resources are needed to leverage additional Fast Passing Zones where we currently do not have a competitive advantage, but with enough focus may be able to develop one?

90 Days	Assess how your team and organization views your competition. How does your leadership team behave toward competitive threats and opportunities? What cultural changes should you make as a Practical Growth Leader to heighten the competitive awareness and focus of your organization?

CHAPTER 6

Step 6: Building the Growth Curves

Building on the Hill

A useful tool to organize a business assessment is the traditional lifecycle curve. Practical Growth Leaders have typically become acquainted with this concept in school or other business venues. Almost any business can locate itself somewhere in the growth cycle. Diagnosing your company's maturity level can help not only in refining your strategy, but also can help accomplished Practical Growth Leaders define their priorities and flex their muscles. Never accept a mature position on the growth curve. Practical Growth Leaders must be innovative. They must look for growth opportunities within or adjacent to the core business. These opportunities help the Practical Growth Leader stay focused toward Building on the Hill of the growth curve. If you accept a mature position on the growth curve, you are admitting defeat for your business. I truly believe that. Innovative solutions around new products, services, competitive points of leverage and a relentless customer focus are critical ingredients that will help you stay on the growth side of the hill.

Concept 6.1

Building on the Hill Practical Growth Concept

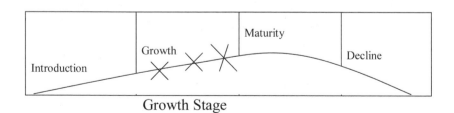

Growth Stage

Five Growth Stage Questions
Where Are You On The Growth Curve?

For any business, times change like the seasons. Like the four seasons rolling from winter to fall and back again, the seasons of a business reflect its own cycle. As a successful business matures, its early growth creates a foundation for longer term success. Growth continues over time but becomes relatively smaller as an increment of a more mature business, as the foundation expands. The Practical Growth Leader must construct continual interventions to keep this natural process from happening. Where is your business on the growth curve cycle? These questions will help the Practical Growth Leader determine where the business is today.

Growth Stage Assessment

Assessing your business's growth stage and its future growth potential requires a candid and objective understanding of your business. This assessment should incorporate not only an analysis of your company's recent financial performance, but also an appraisal of the external environment in which you are operating. Ask questions such as:

1. Are our customers buying more, the same or less of our products than they were last year? Why?
2. Are we finding it easier or more difficult to acquire customers than earlier?
3. Is our competition improving? Are there industry disruptions coming?
4. Are new substitute products or services coming into the market?
5. Can we increase our prices, or are we forced to compete on pricing too frequently?

These are just a few of the questions Practical Growth Leaders will ask to understand the state of their company's business. Great leaders will then use this information to adjust their style and priorities to the needs of the times in the business.

1. Customer buying momentum

The first step in the assessment model is whether your customers are buying more, the same or less of your product than they were last year. It is critical as you begin this analysis that you understand why customers are behaving the way they are in your category. Remember, just like any sports team, your customer loyalty is always getting better or worse every day. Measuring customer buying momentum quickly is essential to reversing rapidly developing negative trends.

2. Easier or more difficult to acquire new customers

As your business matures, the availability of new business becomes more difficult and the cost of acquiring new customers becomes more expensive. Customers are more fragmented than ever before (e.g. watching over 300 cable channels) making new business acquisition more difficult. For most of us, the best way to grow our business over time is to increase the satisfaction, engagement and loyalty of our current customers.

3. Is our competition improving? Are there industry disruptions coming?

Practical Growth Leaders constantly assess competitive strengths, weaknesses and opportunities. In addition, there is also a need to watch closely for industry disruptions.

For example, Panera Bread Company caused an industry disruption in the casual dining industry. Panera's offers good and healthy food fast and gives its customer control of the dining process. Panera's model has disrupted the casual dining industry as well as the quick service restaurant business. The customer has a new choice that combines control, good food, healthy choices and quick service. Industry disruptions can put pressure on traditional competitors and cause an acceleration of their business into a mature cycle. Panera's has redefined the casual dining industry by changing the customers' consideration set.

4. Are substitute products entering the market?

Categories that have low cost, private label substitutes are usually entering the mature side of the growth curve. Price of the goods and services become more important and true brand differentiation becomes more difficult. Retailers introduce private label brands right next to Folgers, Tylenol, Del Monte and a host of other well known maturing brands.

Substitutes can also enter the market when prices escalate beyond what the market will bear. A great example of this trend is ethanol and the role it is playing in gasoline. Ethanol plants are redefining the landscape of rural America all across the plains states. The rural economies of Kansas, Nebraska,

Iowa and many other states are being reshaped by this trend. As the price of gasoline escalates, this trend will continue. It will result in higher prices for grain, corn and feed which will result in higher food prices and a significant relief in fuel prices. The jury is still out on the long-term impact of ethanol. At best, it appears to be a mixed bag of positive and negative outcomes.

5. Can we compete on pricing or are we forced to compete on price too frequently?

As a business matures, price will begin to become a central focus. As more and more lower-price competitors enter the market, your growth will increasingly be at risk. It may no longer be practical to compete on price without seriously eroding margins.

Knowing how to inject innovation into the category at the right time, to move back to the growth side of the curve, is one of the key characteristics of a Practical Growth Leader. Product extensions, additional services and new products to build as well as differentiating your portfolio are critical to your success. Just like a successful television network executive who balances a new line-up every fall, you must create new space for your business and stay several chess moves ahead of the competition. Innovation tied to true customer benefits trumps price almost every time.

Growth Begins With Attitude

Never accept a permanent position for your business on the mature side of the growth curve. Focus on the key interventions to move back to the growth side. Some days, Practical Growth Leaders might feel like they have one foot on the accelerator and one on the brake. Successfully building the growth curves is one of the most difficult challenges to sustaining growth over time. Practical Growth Leaders evaluate their business and adapt their approach to the realities of their situation. As competition in an industry evolves, and a business's maturity evolves, successful Practical Growth Leaders must flex their leadership muscles with interventions to grow.

12 Growth Curve Building Materials

Practical Growth Leaders know how to bring the following twelve building supplies with them to work every day. If you are building a business, utilize these 12 building materials every day to Grow Now! They will work across industries and companies. They will help you to successfully "Build on the Hill" growth side of the curve.

1. Adopt a relentless entrepreneurial spirit
2. Develop a clear and focused vision of the future
3. Show your creative passion and constantly try new things every day
4. Commit to quality that will not be compromised over time
5. Believe in value created by front-line employees
6. Know how to lead change by focusing on the future
7. Anticipate future outcomes
8. Focus on simplified solutions
9. Ask customer questions during Peacetime Interviews
10. Develop rhythm and cadence, utilize humor to lead
11. Focus on building value creation relationships
12. Surround yourself with smarter people who can overcome your personal limitations

1. Relentless Entrepreneurial Spirit

Successful Practical Growth Leaders usually have a relentless entrepreneurial spirit. They bring an over-the-top passion and energy approach to work every day. They are also able to successfully transfer these beliefs and values to their inner circle and front-line troops. Practical Growth Leaders have so much enthusiasm that it spreads to everyone they meet. They have a relentless focus on the need for successful growth. They make decisions with a clear view of both the short-term and long-term implications of their leadership decisions. These leaders play to win and continually are willing to take calculated risks. This is true for a successful Practical Growth Leader for a single owner business or a team leader developing a new growth initiative that will change the future face of a large corporation. In fact, large corporations increasingly value entrepreneurial leadership spirit as a key ingredient for creating a growth culture.

2. Clear and Focused Vision of Future

Practical Growth Leaders have a clear vision of the future and focus their passion and energy only toward those things that will achieve it. Practical Growth Leaders also have the ability to clearly communicate and transfer their future vision into the minds and hearts of those who surround them. They champion their vision every day and positively reinforce the activities needed to achieve it.

Practical Growth Leaders understand that being true to your vision is one of the most important ingredients to achieve successful growth. This is difficult to do because of the temptations that appear every day that entice leaders to alter their vision for growth and success. Most companies who fail become distracted and focus more on the sizzle than the steak of their business.

3. Creative Passion to Try New Things

Why do computers fit into backpacks? Why is Google now a verb rather than just a noun? Why is a .45 considered a gun today rather than a 45 record? Most of these changes took place because Practical Growth Leaders, and the innovators who worked with them, had a creative passion to continually try new things. Trial and error followed by adjustments and more testing with customers is a play book embraced by Practical Growth Leaders. Real generators of growth know that there is honor and celebration in failure as long as it is part of the trial and error journey toward successful growth. Practical Growth Leaders know that to be successful you must test many ideas. They find the leverage points, and launch the successful ones with both speed and agility. Just like the continual coaching adjustments during a football or basketball game, a Practical Growth Leader knows you must try new things every day. You also must be able to capture team learning quickly and adjust on the fly.

4. Quality That Could Not Be Compromised

How do you define quality from a customer perspective? The most important elements of the successful leverage of quality are consistency and predictability. Think of the most powerful customer brands in the world. Brands ranging from Starbucks to Swiffer to McDonald's to Harley Davidson all deliver on the dimensions of consistency and predictability. The same can be said of Tim's Pizza shop. Ultimately, customers don't like surprises. Surprises erode confidence and trust in a given brand. Shareholders also hate surprises. Consistent retail experiences, product reliability, and interactions with customers are cornerstones of successful brands. Predictability also plays a critical role. Customer confidence in what a company will do next adds to the value and equity of their brands.

Consistency and predictability are also critical building materials for Practical Growth Leaders. Think about it. A successful leader is no different than a successful brand. Who likes to work for a leader who surprises you every day? Who wants to work for a growth leader who is inconsistent in how they treat their people? Who wants to work with a leader who is unpredictable in the views and vision for the future? Who enjoys working for a leader who is continually changing objectives and priorities every day? The best leaders rarely ask surprising questions. Their people usually know exactly what to expect every day.

Predictability and consistency are cornerstones of successful Practical Growth Leaders. In fact, without these characteristics, you will not be able to be effective leading a dynamic team toward growth.

5. Front-Line Value Creation

Every effective Practical Growth Leader knows that you must interact among the front-line troops.   Practical Growth Leaders know that you must circulate among your front-line employees and customers every day to win. Remember, Lincoln knew it, too! You're not managing by just walking around. You must listen, ask questions, verify your understanding, and respond with action. If you do, your front-line troops will take any hill to help you achieve your growth plans. If you isolate yourself away from the front-line troops, you will begin to create alternative views of reality among your leadership team. This is very dangerous.

6. Leading Change Effectively

The most important attribute in leading change is simple. You must follow the Five Ps of creating a culture of change:

- Play to win by allocating resources against the greatest points of leverage. You win by focusing your resources against the key strengths you have and at the same time expose the relative weaknesses of your competition. The Fast Passing Zones concept highlighted in Step 5 drives home how to play to win every day.

- Passion to create a change of pace fast enough to push the outer comfort zone of the organization. The pace of change and the speed must be fast enough to transform your organization. Remember, people generally don't like to change. They see it as a risk and will have a natural response to push back. The successful Practical Growth Leader knows that the best way to create the right culture is to make the risk associated with not changing higher than taking the chances associated with the transformation.

- Persuasion to effectively sell the need, opportunities and solutions that drive sustainable change. Persuasion along with the ability to make the case for transformation is critical to create a culture of change. I cannot tell you how many terrible business ideas that were not even worthy of consideration I have seen effectively communicated and sold by great presenters at high levels of major corporations. I consider myself to be a highly effective speaker and presenter who can build a case to move forward on almost any topic. It is important to remember that in the end, only content is king, and style points mean nothing. That said, once a business case is made and the decision to move forward is complete, a powerful story that is effectively shared with your employees will be key to having your team believe they can win.

- Patience to allow different personality types and different parts of the organization to have a different cadence toward change. Everyone does not embrace change at the same rate. A Practical Growth Leader needs to help and support those who embrace change quickly and tolerance to "bring the rest of the team along." If you fail to exercise patience, you may lose some of the key high performers who have a slower cadence toward change, but are critical to a successful transformation. Practical Growth Leaders who lack this patience will ultimately fail because they will lose many of their best people who have slower cadence toward change and need more time to get there.

- Planning is important in a stable and predictable environment. Planning is critical and must be done in more frequent intervals to effectively lead a faster pace of change. Watching game film analyzing what went well and what went wrong today, yesterday, last week or last month is critical in an environment surrounded by change. The need to develop contingency plans up front with dates, gates, and trigger points to implement them often separates the effective Practical Growth Leaders from the pretenders. Sometimes, the key to business growth is how well you handle Plan B. We often asked the objective question: Did we win this week or not? If we won this week, did we achieve success? If we lost, what will make next week have a different and better outcome?

7. Anticipating Future Outcomes

Effective Practical Growth Leaders play chess, not checkers. They plan six to eight moves ahead, rather than one or two. You have to think ahead. Practical Growth Leaders see this raw fact: One out of every five homes bought today is purchased by a single women. They instantly begin to think of the possibilities. They write raw facts down on a blank sheet of paper and begin to play three dimensional chess that involves outcomes and implications. This is usually the difference between winning and losing your quest for real growth. Playing chess without boundaries enables you to imagine the possibilities that transform raw facts into breakthrough growth platforms.

8. Focus on Simplifying Solutions

Have you ever been in a business meeting when the more someone attempts to explain his or her position, the more complicated the issue becomes? Did you ever sit in a university professor's lecture that became more complicated and difficult with each passing minute? The art of simplifying issues into what football coaches often call manageable chunks of yardage is critical to the success of the Practical Growth Leader. For example, Wal-Mart became the world's largest retailer on the simple customer promise of everyday low prices. That is a simple concept that works best when you break it down to its simplest form. Marketers create problems when they add complicated layers on top of a simple and powerful fundamental growth strategy.

Tony Blair, the former Prime Minister of the United Kingdom, offered a great perspective on how to simplify an issue. When asked why he believed so much in America, Blair replied, "A simple measure of a country is how many people want in and how many people want out." Practical Growth Leaders can apply that same logic when taking a simple measure of their company. Great leaders simplify business issues every day. They resist explanations that revolve around complexity. If you think about original customer insights that really drive your business, they are usually the ones right in front of us viewed through a different lens. The programs that are launched to the marketplace that carry complexity as a characteristic almost always fail. Simplifying the business almost always results in better execution. Leaders who embrace implementation as a core competency understand the importance of simplifying the value chain. Leaders who only focus on strategy are destined to create volumes of binders in their office full of all their insightful visions for the future with no measurable results on the scoreboard.

9. Ask Customer Questions

Practical Growth Leaders must spend time with the customer every day to keep their finger on the pulse of the business. What do customers like and why? What are customers requesting that we don't have? What are customers saying about our competition? What do our customers not like about our offering and why? How does our plan for next week, next month, and next year respond to these questions with tangible solutions designed to drive growth? There is no activity that a leader can do every day that is more important than asking customers questions. In many organizations, top leaders are often insulated from direct contact with the customer and too heavily rely on their sales organization and retail groups to provide fighter protection and fly interference.

This can lead to the top executives having information filtered from them by their leadership team who manages the flow of "what matters." This is a recipe for disaster. It can lead to senior executive decision making based on incomplete or inaccurate marketplace and customer information.

10. Develop Rhythm and Cadence

Practical Growth Leaders must develop a rhythm and cadence. There are times to press your advantage. There are also times to go faster and slower. If you push too hard to develop a strategic alliance, it may dissolve in your hands. Many ineffective leaders want to succeed so badly they are like a choir member that desperately sings off key at the exact wrong time. Generally speaking, leaders who develop the proper rhythm and cadence are also good collaborators. They ask for the input from those around them and make the right move at the right time. They have the right cadence and rhythm to avoid moving at the wrong time in the wrong direction.

11. Focus on Building Value Creation Relationships

Practical Growth Leaders know that they must utilize a 360 degree value creation approach to relationships to build their business. Are you spending your time with the right people who can actually help you grow your business?

Keep in mind that 95 percent of the mail you receive will not help you grow your business. You should throw away everything but the five percent that will grow your business. Can you easily identify the five percent that really makes a difference? Which pieces of mail (electronic or stamped) will help you build value creation relationships where you can actively grow your business? The same can be said about business relationships you develop every day. You must identify the five percent that really make the difference. You will need to move outside your comfort zone and spend at least 50 percent of your time on those few relationships. Most leaders who fail spend most of their time interacting within their comfort zones with relationships that don't create incremental value for the business. Effective Practical Growth Leaders focus their resources against the value creation relationships that will build growth and ignore almost everything else.

12. Surround Yourself with Smarter People

You must work hard to overcome your own personal limitations to grow. Former President Ronald Reagan once said, "When I meet with my top officials, I don't want to be the smartest man in the room. I want to surround myself with good people." Ultimately, you must do this by hiring people who are much smarter than you in areas where you have weaknesses. You also need to hire people who have strengths that are different from your strengths; people who are diverse in thought and style and different from you as well as each other. This sounds simple, but it is very difficult to execute. The truth is we tend to identify with and are drawn to people who are like us. This is a major trap for the Practical Growth Leader. I can't think of anything worse than a team of 12 Jim Welches stomping around trying to grow the business. Find people who look, act and think differently from you. Find people who possess the 8 Cs of the Practical Growth Leader and the skills to successfully build the life cycle curves.

These 12 building materials of the Practical Growth Leader will help you keep construction booming on the growth side of the hill.

Simple Squared Path to Growth

I reject the notion that businesses should simply accept that they are on the mature side of the growth curve and operate accordingly. This is called "playing not to lose," and will ultimately result in managing yourself and your team out of a business. The Simple Squared concept is a "play to win" approach that recognizes the critical value associated with both rational and emotional leadership in each letter of the concept. The Simple Squared Concept leverages the group process leadership skills of Strategy, Innovation, Motivation, Planning, Leverage and Execution combined with the individual skills of Strength, Implication, Magic moments, Passion, Listening and Emotion. It is a recipe for how to lead a team to keep building on the growth side of the hill. Warren Buffet, the legendary business leader and investor, said, "Business schools reward difficult, complex behavior more than simple behavior. But simple behavior is more effective."

Concept 6.2

Practical SIMPLE SQUARED Growth Concept
GROW YOUR BRAND/GROW YOUR LEADERS
Follow the SIMPLE SQUARED Path to Growth
SIMPLE SQUARED = Rational + Emotional Leadership Connections

S S (Strategy / Strength)		I I (Innovation / Implication)		M M (Motivation / Moment)		P P (Planning / Passion)		L L (Leverage / Listening)		E E (Execution / Emotion)	
Strategic thought creates a new construct.	Find the single greatest strength of each person on your team and put them in a position to succeed.	Innovation brings the strategy alive in new platforms.	Collaborate to discover the implications of your decisions. "Look before you Leap." Most failures in business are due to not considering implications.	Begin with clear objectives for growth and incentives.	Moments in life create super magic. Always be "in the moment" caring about your people.	Plan for success and failure outcomes. Experiment small and scale fast.	Passion and energy are free! Make a choice to bring them with you every day.	Find the 5% that really matters. Only try to lift the 5%. Remember, the other 95% is what is holding you back… it doesn't really matter. Pay attention to the world around you to open new doors to new market opportunities.		98% of growth activities focus on delivering value creation to the customer. Sail the 8 Cs of the Practical Growth Leader and ignite synergies between the five generations to create a growth culture.	

What's Next?

You are ready to take the next step toward becoming a Practical Growth Leader. It is called Speeding With Your Strengths toward growth. It is time to fasten your seat belts. No tickets will be amended! Remember, as Lee Iacocca, the former CEO of Chrysler said, "The speed of the boss is the speed of the team." We will now review how important speed is to the Practical Growth Leader who wants to finish first. Speed is the biggest single difference maker that can set you apart from your competitors.

Are you ready to pass the Step 6 Hurdle Test?

Step 6 Hurdle Test

1. What are the 12 building materials that will help you successfully build the growth curve?
2. What are the five Ps of leading culture change?
3. What do we mean by the phrase "Develop rhythm and cadence?"
4. What are the top five questions to determine where you are on the growth curve?
5. How does the Simple Squared concept make you think differently about your leadership priorities?

90-Day Building the Growth Curves Flex Plan

Time Frame	Activities
30 Days	Rate your team and entire organization (high, medium, low) against the 12 building materials outlined in Step 6 to help you build the growth curves. Which building materials are strengths in your organization? What are the weaknesses? What are the opportunities?
	Assess how much diversity of leadership you have on your team and organization. (Diversity including people of color, cultural, gender, generational, thought process, leadership style, etc.) Where are the diversity gaps in your organization and how will you proactively address them?

60 Days	Develop an assessment of where you are on the growth curve with your business. Does it vary by the major components of your business relative to unit velocity, pricing, customer acquisitions, competition and substitutes?
	Begin to evaluate the opportunities and resources needed to move mature businesses back to the growth side of the curve.
	Do you have a leadership team that is stuck only focusing on driving a mature business? Have a two day team growth session to review the business opportunities that would enable your team to break through the mature paradigm.
90 Days	Determine the top three game-changer initiatives to reinvent your business for another growth cycle.
	What internal and external resources are needed for your business to deliver against the top three growth game changers?
	Begin to close the variances of your team's skill sets vs. what is needed to move back to the growth side of the curve. Do you have the internal talent needed to break out of the mature paradigm or do you need outside resources?

CHAPTER 7

Step 7: Speeding With Your Strengths

Writer Oliver Wendell Holmes said, "The greatest thing in the world is not so much where we stand, as in what direction we are moving." I would only add that the speed of that movement is also critically important. Speed has redefined how to achieve success in the marketplace. There is a stronger need than ever before to clearly understand how to win by leveraging your strengths through speed. This can create a marketplace buzz and a feeling where you gain momentum quickly among your customers as well as your competitors. Many great football coaches have said over the years, "There is no substitute for speed." How can Dell build a customized computer in three days? There has been a rapid explosion of capabilities on the internet communicating both critical inventory and ordering information to suppliers in an instant. Dell is able to effectively balance customers' needs for immediate gratification and customized solutions with the effective management of finished goods product. The result is a Dell computer that can be built in 72 hours according to specifications. The rules have changed and will continue to evolve at a faster pace.

Rapidly Emerging Trends/Exponential Rate of Change

The key to leveraging strengths with speed is to find strengths that matter. Many companies invest in speed and technology that doesn't make a critical difference. The very first step in determining the strengths that will make a difference is to pay close attention to the world around you. It will open unexpected doors. There are emerging, rapidly developing trends that are shaping our future landscape. Here are some highlights of changes that are making our future very different over the next several years. After surveying the external landscape, we will look inward to review how our capabilities can be leveraged (if at all) against the following emerging trends.

Big Backlash

There is an emerging trend away from bigger is better along with the growing need for personalization vs. mass-production. Big box stores are experiencing a backlash from customers who are experiencing more and more negative feelings from shopping in an overwhelming mass environment. This will create new opportunities for smaller store footprints with special niches. We are seeing examples of this in the hardware business as ACE and TrueValue Hardware stores compete with their big box competitors. Independent hardware retailers are creating new niches by adding products and services ranging from sharpening businesses to lawn and garden equipment rental, U-Haul rentals, party/event rental and a variety of repair services.

Global Culture Differences and Lost In Translation

The days of a U.S. centric only focus in business are over. More and more we are realizing every day how we are all connected around the globe. For example, a hiccup in China's financial markets can cause turmoil on Wall Street within 24 hours.

The need to understand global cultural differences and sensitivities will be essential to the Practical Growth Leader. If you doubt the need to think and to act globally, consider the following examples of large talented corporations who made marketing blunders on the international stage:

- In Taiwan, the translation of the Pepsi slogan "Come alive with the Pepsi Generation" came out as "Pepsi will bring your ancestors back from the dead."

- Kentucky Fried Chicken's "Finger Lickin' Good" slogan has been used the world over successfully. However, in the Hong Kong market the phrase translated into "Eat Your Fingers Off."

- Rolls Royce introduced a new model in Germany called "Silver Mist." In Germany, this phrase translated into "Silver Droppings."

- Procter & Gamble scored a huge win by merging an original customer insight (cleaning faster) with technology to create Swiffer products which was a runaway success in the U.S. However, the company met stiff resistance introducing Swiffer in Italy where the Italian culture places a less positive view toward cleaning short-cuts to save time.

Procter & Gamble Global Strategy

Procter & Gamble has been very successful in their ability to leverage their global supply chain in effective ways to eliminate redundancies and build a very powerful and efficient worldwide marketing, manufacturing, and distribution network. Procter & Gamble focused on fewer, larger, production and distribution facilities while at the same time leveraging global brands to increase marketing efficiency and effectiveness across product categories and national borders. They utilized an effective global strategy that has generated a sustainable competitive advantage and resulted in substantial top-line and bottom-line growth.

Women's Decision-Making Growing

The impact of women in the marketplace is a critical trend that needs to be a key part of the Practical Growth Leader playbook. As pointed out earlier, one out of every five homes is purchased by a single woman. Women make at least 70+ percent of the family purchase decisions, and over 50 percent of the women in the United States live alone. This translates into an emerging and increasingly powerful market segment which we explored in detail as part of Step 4.

Technology Levels Playing Field

Technology has created a level playing field and created a new era in marketing. It has improved the underdog odds in David vs. Goliath match-ups. A few key people with the right computer equipment can quickly produce high quality sales pieces, brochures and newsletters that would have required a full-service major advertising agency to execute only a few years ago. Consider the case of Central Valley Ag in O'Neill, Nebraska. CVA is a sizeable Agricultural Coop that has its worldwide marketing headquarters located in Oakland, Nebraska which has a population of around 1,300 people. However, Marketing Vice-President Reed Nelsen and his small staff put out a consistently high level of creativity and quality of newsletters, brochures and sales pieces that would rival many major agencies. Reed's creative instincts combined with his powerful technology capabilities level the playing field for Central Valley Ag to create more high quality and strong impact materials with less resources required.

Technology Applied to Your Dashboard (Points of Leverage)

Technology has also contributed to a fast break speed of information flow to leaders. The key is to have the right dashboard so you can use technology to see the marketplace and your internal operations with ruthless objectivity against measures that matter. Unfortunately, technology has also led to data overload. Executives today are inundated with thousands of pieces of unconnected data every day. Practical Growth Leaders who build a dashboard of three to five points that are critical to the business will leverage technology to make fast-break decisions to gain a substantial competitive advantage. The Practical Technology Leverage Concept highlights the increasingly meaningful impact of technology in an organization (see below):

Concept 7.1

Practical Technology Leverage Concept

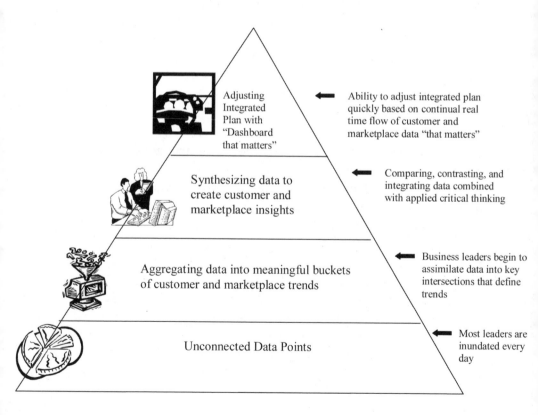

Adjusting Integrated Plan with "Dashboard that matters" ← Ability to adjust integrated plan quickly based on continual real time flow of customer and marketplace data "that matters"

Synthesizing data to create customer and marketplace insights ← Comparing, contrasting, and integrating data combined with applied critical thinking

Aggregating data into meaningful buckets of customer and marketplace trends ← Business leaders begin to assimilate data into key intersections that define trends

Unconnected Data Points ← Most leaders are inundated every day

Reverse Mentoring

Do not underestimate the power of reverse mentoring where tech savvy Millennials and late Generation Xers can help leverage technology in new ways as well as help Baby Boomers assimilate the skills they need to be more speed focused with technology themselves. This reverse mentoring process can work very well as a bridge of synergy across the generations. The fact is Millennials and Generation Xers have a much better perspective on new technologies than Baby Boomers. Find ways to leverage this capability across your entire work team.

Luxury is Becoming More Accessible.

You can now buy plasma TVs in select Wal-Mart stores. You can easily buy expensive cars and homes on the internet and secure the financing on-line as well. I interviewed a mortgage provider that has made $500,000 loans on-line without ever even personally meeting the loan applicants. And most individuals will brag about their great buy. Wouldn't it be great if they were bragging about a great, yet luxurious purchase, from your company?

Saving Has Become More Fashionable

When you attend a dinner party these days, you are likely to hear the host's mention that they got the shrimp from Sam's Club or the Lobster Tails from Costco (along with a bottle of wine). Securing quality products for value prices is now considered chic. My niece proudly proclaimed that she bought her shoes at Target for $12.99. You might not have heard that comment a few years ago. The fashion forward – cheap-chic strategy will cause any focus group of women to smile when the name Target comes out of a research focus group's moderator's mouth. Brands are creating emotional connections all around us. Saving with quality and fashion forward is driving one of those connections.

Growing Need for Safety and Security

Post 9/11 combined with a safety crisis in our schools is changing the face of the Millennial Generation. They feel much less safe and more in need of reassurance than prior generations. Security systems (home and mobile) will rapidly grow in the next five years. The Millennial Generation views terrorism and school safety as their chief concerns. High school and college students now have a much higher anxiety about their day to day safety.

Health and Fitness Focus Continues to Grow

The health/fitness business is exploding with everything from personal trainers, all women exercise facilities, vitamin supplements, and fat free products. The ironic thing is that this is happening when almost 50 percent of kids are suffering from obesity. The average family is eating out three times a week and portions are bigger than ever. This trend is not a fad and will continue to grow as the baby boomers age and we face a national health care crisis. In order to open my own speaking and consulting business, I had to lose 70 pounds to handle the physical demands and to improve my overall health and presence on stage. Baby Boomers, like me, are now faced with critical health choices. Fitness centers and healthy choices will dominate our life in the next decade.

Organic and Natural Trend

The organic and natural trend will continue to emerge. The emphasis on providing healthy food choices and toward recycling and other environmental friendly activities will continue to grow. Customers are embracing the organic trend and brands are steam-rolling their Green solutions into the marketplace. According to a recent issue of BrandWeek, brands including Gerber, Hunts, Ragu, Swanson and Frito Lay are now offering green product alternatives. The long-term impact on the food business will be profound and reshape the shelves over time at your local favorite supermarket. Wal-Mart, Whole Foods and Starbucks lead the way of companies the public associates with green reputations and environmental responsibility.

On-line Has Gone Mainstream

Surfing the internet is now the number one distraction at work. While people are communicating and surfing the net more than ever before, a feeling of isolation is growing and people are increasingly left alone in the dark late at night in front of a computer screen. Google has become a verb and information access has exploded throughout every dimension of our culture. My father's generation's idea of sacrifice was working road construction in Illinois during the Depression for $3 a day. Now, if my son's latest I-Pod or video game takes too long to upload, it is unacceptable for his generation. The internet has raised response time expectations for customers and clients. On-line going mainstream means customers expect real time responses and immediate gratification. This will have a major impact on how growth leaders lead the Millennial generation.

It is a technology-dependent generation that has a short internet focused attention span. Interactive business training by companies using video game technology will be a field of rapid growth going forward.

Marketing/Revolution

Marketing will be completely redefined in the coming years. It is estimated that over 50 percent of all homes in the United States will have TIVO and DVR within the next few years. The value of the 30-second commercial is plummeting as you read this chapter. Companies are migrating dollars away from television toward more print, on-line and grass roots marketing. From Procter & Gamble to Starbucks to Wal-Mart, the future battle ground of marketing will be on every street corner of the world. Customer relationship management will move more granular and the product mix by individual rooftop will vary dramatically. Restaurant menus will have real differences in chains across America reflecting the changing faces of our culture. The biggest challenge companies will face as marketers is to pursue rooftop customization while protecting profitability. This has caused many customers to develop tailored templates of store types that are scaleable. Marketers who crack the code that allows for neighborhood customization with scaleable solutions that profitably grow revenue will be the big growth winners. Companies that maximize customization with solutions that are not scaleable or come forward with more general solutions that are imposed across rooftops will be the big losers. This tightrope will be the biggest obstacle to retail growth in the next five years.

Generational Differences Emerging Fast

The differences between the generations are continuing to increase every day. Baby Boomers and Generation Jonesers who together control over 70 percent of the wealth in the U.S. will become increasingly important market segments as they reach into their fifties and sixties. As pointed out in Step 4, you will see more and more products and services marketed directly to these two separate and distinct generations.

These generational differences are increasingly causing "sparks" in the workplace. Baby Boomers are wondering about the work ethic of the Millennial Generation. Generation X employees are increasingly resenting their Baby Boomer bosses who sometimes rely too heavily on relationships and emotion vs. fact-based decision making. Millennials are wondering about their fulfillment as they long to be part of something that speaks to a higher mission of why they come to work every day. Baby Boomers wonder why performance reviews with Generation Xers often feel like ongoing employment negotiations. The workforce composition is rapidly changing and the attitude of your teams right along with it.

Speeding with Strengths Winners

There are several successful brands and companies that leverage their greatest strengths by finding their PAC Power and by bringing creative as well as superior solutions to the marketplace in response to the customer needs that matter most. They consistently focus their resources where they have the most leverage.

Winning on Every Street Corner

A new Walgreens store opens approximately every 20 hours in the United States. Walgreens has cracked the code on how to move with speed and operational excellence in the convenience chain drug space. The Walgreens' philosophy is to have over 7,000 Walgreens stores by 2010 (many 24 hours). Their strategy is to get people in and out of the stores quickly every day. Walgreens' gift back to the customer is a very precious asset called time. It is all about convenience and leveraging technology to create a single customer link and experience across the Walgreens' Brand. They understand the business they are in and have a singular focus to grow it every day.

Approximately 138 million people a week go to Wal-Mart, which represents almost 50 percent of the U.S. population. Wal-Mart focuses on customer check-out experience ratings in its weekly meetings. Wal-Mart uses speed and operational excellence to deliver those numbers every week. Wal-Mart reviews how to improve its check-out customer experience every day.

McDonald's continues to win with speed and operational excellence. McDonald's serves over 50 million customers every day worldwide in 119 countries and has over 30,000 retail locations. McDonald's combines speed, operational excellence and consistency to deliver these numbers. The business was built on the premise that a Big Mac in Seattle will taste just like the one you order in Omaha or New York City. This brand was built on speed and consistency.

Redefining a Category

Starbucks has plans to open 40,000 retail outlets worldwide and redefined the coffee category through leveraging product innovation and a unique retail experience. Starbucks has become a gathering place where people come together every day to order, "My Starbucks." When people go to Starbucks and order coffee, they use a language that did not exist 10 or 20 years ago. Coffee had been a declining category for a long time. Starbucks cracked the coffee code using product innovation, quality and consistency inside a unique gathering place. Starbucks has a very small national marketing media budget. It relies on product innovation, employees and retail experience. It is also important to note how Starbucks has used its employer branding to create engagement and loyalty. People enjoy working at Starbucks and they continue to be proud of the brand association long after they leave the company.

New Customer Insights

Procter & Gamble created and launched Swiffer products by combining original customer insights with a powerful technology capability. CEO A.J. Lafley asked Procter & Gamble executives to actually go out and clean with customers for six months and learn the critical customer insights that would unlock the industry. Procter & Gamble had always run television commercials advertising how their cleaning products always got your house 20 percent cleaner, compared to the competition. Procter & Gamble executives cleaned with customers and learned what was really important to customers was not how much more clean Procter & Gamble products were versus the competition, it was the need to speed up the cleaning process in order to get on with the more important things in their time-pressured lives. For example, cleaning your house in two hours vs. four hours was the critical customer insight benefit. Procter & Gamble leveraged this insight along with unique technology capabilities to create a $300 million-plus new cleaning category.

Brand Quality and Emotional Connection

Harley-Davidson leveraged product quality with innovation to create a unique emotional connection with their brand. The improvement in product quality and innovation created an emotional connection with their brand that is extremely powerful today. Can you think of any brand that has a more powerful emotional connection than Harley-Davidson? It reminds me of the old story of the chicken and the pig. When you enjoy an eggs and bacon breakfast, it is important to remember that the chicken participated. But the pig was committed. I think on the continuum of participation vs. commitment – Harley brand fans are partial to hogs. When people often wear your brand name on their bodies, I call that a personal commitment.

Speeding With Your Strengths Benefits

It is critical as a Practical Growth Leader that you identify your core competencies and rapidly accelerate how fast you leverage your strengths. There are critical benefits that support the Speeding With Your Strengths strategy!

1. It will force you to drive toward simplifying the value chain and reducing costs. If you don't, you will lose your leadership market position and profitability over time.

2. You will anticipate customer needs faster and lead quickly to customer solutions staying one step ahead of the competition. Once a customer starts singing that old Beatles song... "Help, I need somebody," you are in trouble! Staying ahead of customers' attitudes and loyalty on a real time basis is critical to a Practical Growth Leader. Customer feedback systems that provide immediate, direct feedback that can result in a quick corrective action are becoming much more applicable in today's marketplace with current technology. For example, the ability to flag problems with a new program launch on day one can dramatically increase the speed of your customer recovery plan and reduce the costs of execution problems. Companies that lead these new systems with "real time" customer feedback will enjoy a sustainable competitive advantage over companies that cling to the traditional periodic customer survey mechanisms of the past.

3. Speeding With Your Strengths helps you to out flank your competition and keep your brand more relevant with customers. Playing offense with the competition is much more fun than playing defense. Leveraging speed will keep your competitors guessing what you will do next.

4. The other key benefit is the ability to test ideas small, learn quickly and scale fast to drive growth. Many large companies have been historically too slow to test and roll-out scaleable solutions. This has enabled

competitors to outflank their tests and move forward with marketplace speed as well as effectiveness building market share that is difficult to challenge going forward.

5. Speeding With Your Strengths will move your employee engagement and commitment to a higher level. Everyone wants to win. Employees will embrace speed as a play to win tactic and will be highly motivated to deliver creative solutions to the marketplace that result in the company winning, building their skill sets portfolio and the feeling that they are making a difference every day. Speeding With Your Strengths brings energy to your culture. It will encourage your team to be bold and take calculated risks. Speed will support momentum and help convert the Building Inspectors into Practical Growth Leaders, as well as convert the Bad News Employees and Turtles in Their Shells into helpers. The Painful Porcupine will become frustrated and leave your company or burrow deep into bunker mentality. Speed kills inertia and atrophy. Speed also helps kill fear while building team confidence.

Summary

Speeding With Your Strengths works for organizations and teams. When building effective teams, ask each member to highlight his or her single greatest individual strength. Integrate and add up those collective individual strengths in front of the entire team. It will be an impressive list which will illustrate the individual talents showcased by each team member. Utilize the collective individual strengths as key inputs to help define the single greatest strength of your team. You are well on the way toward Speeding With Your Strengths. It is all about matching your greatest strength where you have the most leverage and adding speed just like you add the straw that stirs the drink.

What's Next?

Experienced teams need to recommit to new speed oriented playbooks with creative solutions. The next step of our Practical Growth Leadership journey will highlight how to turbo charge your teams so they can adjust their sails to win! We will also look in the mirror at the brick wall barriers inside you and your organization that can stop growth right in its tracks. These dirty dozen barriers are the biggest challenge to the Practical Growth Leader.

Step 7 Hurdle Test

1. Which rapidly emerging trends highlighted are the most likely to directly impact your business?
2. What trends exist that you can leverage quickly with one of your core capabilities?
3. Which Speeding With Your Strengths benefits has the most application for your company?
4. What are the barriers in your business that get in the way of Speeding With Your Strengths?
5. What are the common characteristics of successful companies that speed with their strengths?

90-Day Speeding With Your Strengths Flex Plan for Growth

Time Frame	Activities
30 Days	Develop a one-page position paper highlighting the top three strengths of your business.
	How important are these three strengths to your key customers (high, medium, low)?
	On a scale of zero to five, with five being outstanding, rate the speed of delivery that these three strengths support your marketplace value chain.
60 Days	Determine the top three trends that you can leverage in your business.
	Assess your current expertise and capabilities to respond to these external trends.
90 Days	Peacetime Customer Interviews assess strengths.
	Work directly with your customers to co-evaluate and co-discover the mutual market opportunities and set priorities for the ones to go after first. Your customers will help you set your priorities.
	Begin to "test small" against the top opportunities with the capability to scale fast to be first to market.

CHAPTER 8

Step 8: Adjusting Your Sails to Win

The Enemy Is Us

Winning the growth race is similar to chasing America's Cup. Ray Davies, Strategist, Emirates Team New Zealand, once said during a Louis Vuitton Cup semi-finals race: "It was tough to keep close, defend and back yourself. We felt we had to keep the hammer on and keep them boxed in. These conditions made it difficult, they got back into us, especially in that last run and we are happy to come out on top." How do you adjust your sails to win the race in your company or organization? There are several dimensions involved when adjusting to change in the external marketplace, customer priorities and competition. Unfortunately, the biggest barriers to growth live inside your team and organization. They are the limits or constraints you place on each other and your teams which inhibit sustainable growth. These growth barriers must be knocked down in order to achieve breakthrough growth. The following 12 reefs and construction zones stand between you and your team achieving your growth objectives. They are highlighted in The Dirty Dozen Practical Growth Triangle concept.

Just as many planes and ships have disappeared over the years in the Bermuda Triangle, the same vanishing act will happen to your practical growth plans if you fail to navigate around the Show Stoppers found in The Dirty Dozen Growth Triangle Concept.

Concept 8.1

"The Dirty Dozen" Growth Triangle Concept

1. Core Capabilities Not Aligned to Growth

One of the biggest challenges faced by many companies and organizations is that they have a mismatch between the core capabilities they currently have and the ones they need to sustain future growth. No matter how much they put the hammer down on the growth engine, they simply do not have the horsepower to deliver the goods. At the end of the day, when companies stray too far away from their core competencies, this is a common outcome. The company is then faced with the painful decision of whether or not to acquire the additional capabilities to grow their business. This is why the PAC Power model introduced in Step 4 is so important to your leadership team. The PAC Power concept overlay helps you search for closer-in growth opportunities that leverage core capabilities you already have in your organization. Your chances of winning are improved when you Speed with your Strengths utilizing PAC Power.

2. No Top Down Focus On Growth

What percentage of CEO time is spent every week engaged in core growth initiatives? The answer to this question will go a long way toward determining whether or not your organization is truly committed to growth. Many companies talk a good game about growth, but the true indicator is how much time the CEO and leadership teams actually spend on the topic. Develop a 30-day log book for your company keeping track of how many hours you and your team actually spend on growth initiatives every month. This will separate the true Practical Growth Leaders from the executives who "look good and smell good" in meetings. If you and your team are not talking about and doing things every day to drive growth, then your top down commitment is nothing more than optics.

There are key indicators to look at closely when evaluating whether or not an organization has a growth passion with teeth in it. First of all, do growth measures represent at least 50 percent of senior executives' performance objectives and compensation? If the answer to this question is no, you are only paying lip service to driving growth. If you fail to tie growth measures directly to your team's individual and group evaluations, you will not create a focus around driving incremental business. If you do not tie senior leaders' compensation, including bonus and a discretionary portion of their base salary increase to achieving growth objectives, you will have a management team that focuses on the day-to-day operational issues facing the business which rarely create growth.

Second, are there common growth objectives that motivate your leaders to collaborate closely together across key functions to drive growth? If the answer to this question is no, you are a growth pretender and not a contender. Business is full of average companies that are primarily driven by individual division or even department objectives with no real common measures. This is a roadmap to total disaster over time with civil war out-breaks involving your leadership teams. Finally, your growth objectives should be aligned closely with the growth of your clients and/or customers. Your culture to drive growth along with your line of sight should be directly tied to your customer segments.

3. Failure to Face Reality Together

Dolly Parton, the famous country music singer said, "We cannot direct the wind, but we can adjust the sails." True leaders must first agree on the direction of the wind. One of the top killers of growth in any organization is when your leadership team is not on the "same page" relative to the problems facing the business and the solutions needed to grow. These alternative views of reality grind growth to a halt and destroy teams faster than almost anything else. How do you know whether or not you and your team have a similar view of reality? Ask your leadership team five questions to measure the consistency of your vision of the future:

- Do we agree on the top two high potential growth intersections facing our business?
- What are the top two challenges or threats that could negatively impact growth for our business in the future?
- How big (revenue and profit) will we be 60 months from right now?
- What should we be doing to grow the business?
- What business activities should we stop doing and reallocate those resources toward growth?

If your leadership team has significantly different answers to these five Practical Growth Leader questions, you do not have a shared vision for growth. Chances are that you also may have a culture where finance blames sales who holds marketing accountable, who in turn, lashes out at front-line employee execution as possible reasons for not achieving their common business growth objectives. Many capable individual leaders have failed as a team player because they could not agree on a growth vision for the company. It is critical that you ask these five questions both individually and collectively to your team members. Then you must identify the gaps, and resolve your differences pertaining to your company's or organization's growth vision. It will not be easy, but it will be worth it.

4. Saving Your Way To Winning

One of the most difficult things to do as a leader is to invest in the future by taking a short-term profit hit on the bottom-line. This takes a great deal of courage. It is much easier to satisfy associates, customers and shareholders by not rocking the boat, continuing a steady and predictable profit stream while not investing enough in future growth. Think about how Wall Street is wired. The entire stock market lives quarter to quarter and is unforgiving in its assessment of profit results. Are you consistently making your own profit numbers and falling short of your annual revenue goals every year? If the answer to this question is yes, then by definition, you are Saving Your Way to Winning.

This will result in the slow and painful death of your company. The best way to overcome this position is to share the long-term perspective of the impact of this strategy. Utilize a 60-month timeline and ask the following questions:

- What is our projected market share in five years?
- How large will we be in revenue in the next five years?
- What will be the condition/value of our current assets in five years?
- What competitive threats may emerge as a result of under-investing in the business over time?
- What changes are we making to hit next year's revenue number?
- What is our five-year capital investment strategy for growth?
- Are we continuing to reduce costs in revenue generating assets (e.g. product and service development, sales, marketing) versus focusing on non-revenue generating areas which might accelerate the decline in growth?

It is critical that you lift the leadership words and deeds above the tyranny of quarterly earnings. A well-defined vision is imperative. Along with supporting growth plans and specific implementation initiatives, this will increase leadership confidence in taking a longer term perspective, while investing in growth.

5. Playing Not to Lose

Some management teams are unwilling to take the risks that are essential to play to win. A risk adverse leadership team will stall growth over time. What does this look like in an organization? The Playing Not to Lose disease takes on the following symptoms:

- Decision process is slow, involving several layers and ad hoc committees.
- Accountabilities are spread thinly through teams and committees so no one person is responsible for delivering results.
- Decisions are changed multiple times, after they are made the first time.
- Leaders demonstrate a Turtles-Hiding-In-Their-Shells mentality and are not comfortable taking unpopular positions.
- Passive/aggressive behavior dominates your landscape. Managers say negative things about other leaders and functions in private discussions, which are never openly or publicly aired in the company during critical decision times.

Playing Not to Lose creates a mindset that is very dangerous to growth. It is like a football team that goes into a prevent defense with one quarter left and a 17-point lead only to wind up losing by three points on a last-second field goal. The prevent defense prevents you from winning the football game. Playing Not to Lose in business will prevent you from winning and growing. The best way to break out of this mess is to create pockets of Playing to Win teams within your company and reward their operating style and results in front of the rest of the organization. In addition, third-party, outside-culture interventions are needed to rebuild and refocus the teams to Play to Win with positive, supportive and contagious behavior. It is also important that you clearly establish accountability and individual consequences for achieving performance objectives and transforming each leader's personal style. Some will make it and some will not. The key is to make the assessment quickly and move swiftly to replace ineffective leaders who continue the Playing Not to Lose leadership behaviors.

6. Hockey Stick Growth Models

Beware of new business growth models that have a five-year growth curve that looks like a hockey stick with all the results back-end loaded. Hockey stick projections show little or no growth in the early years and then take off with rapid growth in the later time frames. These models are a recipe for disaster. They involve making large up-front capital investments with almost no incremental profit return for 48 to 60 months. The way to address this is to make smaller investments up front to test small and scale large. That strategy will put your company on a fast track toward success. The other avenue is to simply approve a limited number of hockey stick plans in your growth portfolio. Insist that your teams invest in fast break growth opportunities and keep the number of hockey sticks you approve few and far between each other. You should have plans in your portfolios that focus on closer in-growth opportunities. Otherwise, you wind up investing up front to chase 48- to 60-month rainbows with no pot of gold as a reward. There is also a tendency to stay with these hockey stick plans too long, thus losing even more capital investment dollars and profit. Don't stick with the plan for too long a period of time. It reminds me when a manager leaves his starting pitcher in the game too long and they get knocked all over the park. The end result is a loss. In business, you can lose your company. It is critical that you make the call and avoid leaving your leadership team on a growth initiative that is not delivering the goods. One of the most important skills of The Practical Growth Leader is the willingness to admit - and even embrace - failure. When you do this, you will quickly capture learning that will lead to future growth.

7. Growth Plans Not Aligned to Customers (Granularity)

Are your growth plans aligned with your critical customer segments? What is your rate of current and new customer growth? How do these customer segments overlay against your portfolio of products and services? Can your leaders articulate how they will achieve a growth objective? For example, if an annual 12 percent growth rate is the target; can your leaders outline the role each key component will play in achieving the objective? Practical Growth Leaders understand the granularity of their growth plans and can articulate clearly where the significant chunks of the 12 percent increase will come from to achieve the plan. It is critical that Practical Growth Leaders have the discipline to make this analysis happen. Then, as Practical Growth Leaders we put plans in place to address the gaps. Most companies have high, lofty growth plans. The problem is they often move from these high level objectives to become mired in executional details. Many organizations miss the critical middle step of breaking down high-level growth objectives into manageable chunks of growth. These can be identified and measured over time, resulting in corrective action as needed. Critical questions every Practical Growth Leader should ask are: Where will the key components of this growth objective come from within the business? Do these plans align with your customer segments and their growth potential?

8. Treat All Customers the Same

How do you invest in your customers? If you treat all your customers the same, you will fail to sustain growth. Practical Growth Leaders who are successful know that they must invest in customers differently based on the following key variables:

- Revenue and profitability results and future potential
- Risk associated with losing the customer's loyalty
- Level of complexity – more complex customers require more resources
- New customers that can be acquired as part of your core business vs. long shots who are unlikely to fall your way
- Top customer segments that are being targeted by your competitors require more attention vs. segments your rivals are ignoring

Utilize these dimensions as a screening process to place your customer segments in different buckets, based on their incremental growth potential as well as downside risk.

9. Out-of-Control Growth

One way to derail your plans quickly is to focus exclusively on creating a culture focused on sustaining growth without supporting systems and operational support. One of the most important things successful Practical Growth Leaders must be able to do is to establish strong collaboration with their development and operational teams. The technology and operations teams are like the air traffic controllers of a major airport. If they are not linked with your growth plans, your team and your customers will have a mess on their hands. Companies who fail to do this will wind up like the German Army in the World War II Battle of the Bulge. They simply ran out of gas and were easily defeated by the allies. If a company grows too rapidly without systems and operations support, the organization will run out of gas and their growth plans will never come to fruition. This often happens during the early growth stage of the business life cycle. One of the most important skill sets of "Building the Growth Curves" is to build in systems and operational support that will rapidly grow successfully with a healthy top and bottom line.

10. Resources Not Aligned With Growth

What percentage of your total resources are committed to growth initiatives? Do you have the right leadership talent, physical assets and financial resources to deliver against your organizations growth objectives? How do you manage your core repeat business effectively while you chase "Gold Growth Segments?" One common mistake organizations make is to have lofty growth goals that are not appropriately resourced underneath the strategic plan. Take a resources inventory and make sure you have sufficiency in people talent, physical assets and financial resources to support granular, manageable chunks of growth.

11. Narrowly Defined Industry Definition

Are you in the video business or the entertainment business? Are you in the travel industry or do you make memories that last a lifetime? Disney is not just about theme parks, rides, characters and products. Disney is "Where Magic

Begins." How do you define your business? Where do your boundaries start and stop? Many organizations make the critical mistake of defining their business too narrowly in their growth plans. This can "screen off" substantial growth opportunities that are directly adjacent to your core business. Your leadership team should bring in outside talent and perspective to facilitate this discussion. You and your team are too close to your organization and industry to do major surgery on yourselves. You will need some outside expertise to help you take the blinders off, broaden the definition of your playing field and identify new growth platforms that are part of or directly adjacent to your core business.

12. Unable to Identify How to Leverage Key Growth Drivers

Where are you investing to grow your business? If you had one more dollar to spend, would you put it in innovation, customer loyalty, sales support or financial/operational systems? Where is the leverage for the greatest growth return? Identify the growth intersections by utilizing PAC Power and chase the Gold Growth Segments by investing where you have the greatest leverage. It is also important to understand the leverage points that matter to consistently drive sustainable growth. Many organizations make the mistake of investing heavily in functions that do not directly impact growth. Any time an investment decision is reviewed for your approval, ask a critical question. For every dollar I choose to invest in this initiative, what will I receive in incremental hard growth dollars to the top and bottom line? If you cannot get a straight answer with accountability, do not spend the money.

"Dirty Dozen" Summary

At the end of the day, your ability to successfully adjust your sails to navigate around the 12 reefs and barriers outlined in this chapter will play a large role in determining whether or not you will be a successful Practical Growth Leader. You will need to be a resilient leader to make it happen with your team and customers. Do you have the passion to keep coming back and asking your team the tough questions? Jon Bon Jovi, the iconic musician, said, "Passion, not pedigree will win in the end." The power to overcome these reefs and construction zones resides in our ability to have a totally consuming passion for growth combined with ruthless objectivity in working through and around The Dirty Dozen barriers. Dangerous politics live within these reefs and barriers. The best way to start is to openly review these 12 Show Stoppers with your team and put the elephants on the table. If you fail to openly address these issues in your organization, they will become a drag on your future growth plans.

Keeping Score – The Practical Growth Leader Dashboard

One of the most critical aspects of an effective Practical Growth Leader is to rally the entire organization around three to five measures that matter. Zig Ziglar, the motivational speaker and author, said, "When you set goals, something inside of you starts saying, 'Let's go. Let's go,' and ceilings start to move up." I would add that it is important to make sure your team is moving the ceiling at the same time and in the same direction. Goals that align cross-purposes with each other can stall growth inside an organization. One of the most important things a Practical Growth Leader can do is make sure everyone gets on board with the top three to five measures that define the organization winning.

The Practical Growth Leader dashboard should summarize a flow of real-time data reflecting how we are doing against these three to five common measures. Variances of actual results vs. our common goals should provide the basis for decisions and action plans. Everyone must agree on what success looks like every day and at the end of the year. This is a major issue in companies that have many measures that point to different conclusions. For example, did this stock number exceed sales expectations or not? If the answer to that question is: It depends on who you ask and what measure they use, then you are in deep trouble.

Unfortunately, this is the answer today in too many companies. The Practical Growth Leader must embrace a culture where everyone agrees to the top three to five growth measures and pursues each one with both an individual and collective passion. We must also all agree and embrace what our collective success looks like going forward.

The Practical Growth Leader dashboard should be reviewed every day regardless of your industry, size of company and unique business challenges. It is also important that everyone from the security guard to the head of marketing to the administrative assistants to the CEO can all easily understand and explain our progress toward achieving these three to five dashboard measures. This is how you create and sustain a culture with a true passion for growth. Companies that consistently win talk about their dashboard measures every day, and how they can impact future growth. Here is a good litmus test. Ask five to 10 people across your organization at various levels about the critical measures for success at your company. If you get inconsistent feedback, you will not be able to achieve and sustain real growth over time.

Rapid Growth Strike Force

David Ogilvy, the advertising legend and top executive, once said, "A well run restaurant is like a winning baseball team. It makes the most of every crew member's talent and takes advantage of every split-second opportunity to speed up service." Do you have a rapid strike force that can speed up growth on a key initiative? When you discover leverage points to grow effectively in your organization, can you quickly reallocate resources to go after the opportunity? Most companies fail to assume the growth leadership position because they are not wired for true speed. They rely on their organization structure and the chain of command to drive their business. How would you feel if your top competitor embraced a Rapid Growth Strike Force model starting tomorrow morning? My guess is you would have an upset stomach and probably reach for a large roll of Tums. If that is true, why not seize the moment to put your competition in the same position. Effective Practical Growth Leaders see a key growth opportunity and strike quickly to move the ball down the field against their competition. A Rapid Growth Strike Force of key leaders can accelerate growth quickly on key growth initiatives and leave your competitors out of position and caught off-guard. A critical component to a Play to Win growth strategy is to Speed with your Strengths by quickly redeploying key people and physical assets to rapidly scale emerging growth opportunities. Companies that do it finish first. Companies who are slow to respond to these points of leverage fall further behind the leaders. The Practical Growth Leader Strike Force can also create high energy for growth in your organization and a feeling that you are coming to work everyday as part of a winning team.

What Does The Strike Force Look Like?

Temporary cross-development teams that are created for a concentrated period of time, focused on a specific growth initiative, are the best way to drive Rapid Growth Strike Force momentum. These Practical Growth Leader strike forces should be formulated utilizing the following 5-point methodology:

1. The cross-development team should temporarily report directly to the CEO and his or her leadership team. This is critical to make sure the team has the resources it needs and to make sure everyone else stays out of its way. If you have the Growth Strike Force report further down in the organization, failure is likely a pre-determined outcome. The team will almost always be defeated over time by the every-day inertia and politics of any organization.

2. If possible, the percentage of time each cross-development individual team member should spend on the specific growth initiative is a minimum of 50 percent of their time. The most effective cross development growth initiative teams have some team members working on assignments full time. This is to make sure we are moving forward every single day. Otherwise, the team members will become distracted by their day-to-day responsibilities and lose their focus on key growth initiatives.

3. These teams usually can be the most effective when they are created, operationalized, and dissolved in three to six months. Then, the initiative needs to be adapted and embraced by the rest of your organization in order to effectively move forward. This is important because it is difficult for a temporary team to sustain momentum for any longer than 90 to 180 days, and for the initiative to bear fruit, at some point, the rest of the company needs to own it.

4. Team members should have their own cross-development team work location that is outside the daily grind of the offices. Possible locations might include warehouses, garages, rural farms and/or studios where creativity can flourish without being inhibited by the everyday issues associated with running the core business. These off-site locations, which can be built or acquired over time, create a special environment which may include everything from basketball hoops to unique and stimulating art pieces. These facilities should be full of flip charts, masking tape, white boards and even a few laptops. However, be careful about everyone using laptops in this environment. Most innovative ideas that lead to breakthrough growth tend to happen in a high touch, tactile environment. There, people can look at each other eye to-eye, while drawing on ideas together, rather than e-mailing or text messaging each other across the room. This should be an innovative environment where leaders can refuel and focus on their future individual, team and organization growth plans. It is a highly interactive, high energy and challenging environment that is all about providing the leadership that fuels growth.

5. Cross-development teams should represent diversity in their team membership. I define diversity as people of color, gender, thought, style, function and generational. If you walk in to see a cross-

development practical growth team that looks alike, sounds alike and represents only a couple of key functions, you are probably headed for deep trouble on the initiative. People with different perspectives and life experiences have the best chance to come together at the innovation table and deliver breakthrough results.

Growth Strike Force Summary

Nothing creates growth faster than speed and momentum in any organization. The cross-development strike force teams enable you to respond quickly to marketplace changes without having to reorganize your company. It is important to note that these teams will cause friction in your organization. As a Practical Growth Leader, it is critical that you embrace and manage the friction and conflict these teams will create in your organization. If you lead and manage these teams effectively, they will help you transform your total culture into a collective passion for achieving real and sustainable growth.

Third-Party Growth Engagement

One of the critical elements to driving real and sustainable growth is to bring in a third party (e.g. consulting firm) to help reset the table from an outside perspective. There are several key benefits to pursuing an outside resource to help you focus on growth:

1. Third-party interaction can help to stimulate you and your leadership teams thinking in new ways about how to view and leverage the boundaries as well as dynamics of your industry. Don't fall into the trap of developing a narrow view of your business. An outside engagement can help break-down preconceived bias and judgments about your industry and your company's game plan. This can also help you better understand your true competitive set.

2. You are able to bring more objectivity to the issue by avoiding the baggage each internal team member brings to the table. Every division and leader within your organization has an individual agenda. This human behavior is virtually unavoidable. An outside engagement can help you referee some of the issues and put an objective point of view on the table.

3. This will help broaden your perspective on how to view and leverage

your organization's entire value chain. There are some parts of your value chain that you take for granted and do not think about on a regular basis. An outside engagement may identify some new opportunities in the old places on your value chain.

4. Perspectives and best practices from clients in other industries can be brought forward and become part of your future consideration set. One of the biggest discoveries you will make is how similar your issues are to Practical Growth Leaders in other industries.

5. An outside perspective can often help you see that your greatest opportunities are low-hanging fruit that is currently right in front of you and can come alive when it is repositioned, packaged differently or bundled in a new way. This is often the greatest benefit of all because you often see something right in front of you in a very different way.

Third-Party Engagement Cautions

I spent most of my career on the client side, working closely with many outside consultants over the last 30 years. There are some pitfalls to third party consulting engagements that should be considered by any Practical Growth Leader. The following five elements are early warning detectors regarding the true value of your outside engagement:

1. Make sure the third party is focused on growing your business rather than the array of services they provide your organization. Beware of the consulting team that is rapidly attempting to expand its business within your organization before it has had adequate time to learn your business. A proposal for an early expansion is a red flag regarding motive.

2. Be cautious about third-party growth engagements that involve interviews at all levels of your organization that simply lead to a "play back" report of what you already know. I want to be clear here. Interviews up front are critical, but they should lead to creative and original business growth insights, not a book report on the status of your company. Do you have any binders you paid for in your office that have content that only tells you what you already know? That said, I cannot stress enough how important in-depth, one-on-one interviews are to any successful third-party engagement.

3. Beware of third-party engagements that start out with visits from senior vice-presidents of the consulting firm that quickly lead, in a few weeks, to junior people running all over the organization interviewing your people. If the interviews are so critical to the third-party engagement process, the senior leaders should be the ones who conduct them. If you are paying for senior leadership, you need to make sure you are getting it. This issue often surfaces in consulting assignments.

4. Make sure the third-party engagement has an upside incentive tied to a timeframe and performance. A defined incentive helps insure that the critical outside leaders are as motivated to win as you are going forward. If everyone is in the game together, there is a greater passion to grow. A Practical Growth Leader ties a significant portion of the outside fee engagement to performance. This also helps to focus your third-party engagement around generating results. Have you ever hired a consulting firm that sold you a wide array of services, created marvelous power-point presentations, which led to a series of recommendations that added no real value to your business? This often happens when fees are not effectively tied to performance.

5. Most leaders have third-party trust issues that must be overcome. Do some trust testing early in the third-party engagement process to make sure the third-party partner is someone you can trust to be a part of your business landscape. Create deliverables tied to specific dates and outcomes to help to build trust in each other.

Third-Party Engagement – Bottom Line

I truly believe engaging a third-party is a critical element to achieving real and sustainable growth. In addition to considering the variables of the relationship we have already outlined, it is also critical that you target an outside engagement with someone who has different skill sets than your leadership team. For example, if you have a team of great implementers, an outside engagement for strategic input might be very valuable. Conversely, if executional issues and problems are barriers to growth, find an outside team that can bring flawless implementation planning and delivery to the table. The bottom line is third-party engagement should fill in the gaps in your organization while finding the key areas that must be leveraged to drive your business.

Summary

We have reviewed The Dirty Dozen reefs and construction zones that are often Show Stoppers in the Practical Growth Leader's journey toward success. We have also reviewed how a consistent dashboard is essential for you and your team to succeed. In addition, we have outlined a successful game plan to create and form Rapid Strike Growth Teams to lead the transformation of your culture to one with an every day drum beat consisting of passion, energy and enthusiasm to drive growth together. Finally, we have charted a path to engage third-party perspectives and assets from outside the organization to help you and your team focus on how to drive the business in new and creative ways.

What's Next?

Adjusting Your Sails to Win is step No. 8. This step enables you to reach the summit. The next chapter will focus specifically on how to leverage your learning across all 8 steps as well as how to integrate and relate 8 critical concepts along the way with each other. These steps are interlocking and must be integrated together to flex your leadership muscles with maximum strength and effectiveness. While each step has strong individual power, it is the way they are connected together that makes the difference between an effective Practical Growth Leader and one who can lead his or her team to victory every time they take the field.

Before we move forward to integrate the 8 steps, are you ready to clear the final individual step hurdle?

Step 8 Hurdle Test

1. What are the top 12 barriers and construction zones that can grind growth to a screeching halt?

2. Why is a consistent dashboard so important?

3. What are the benefits of the Practical Growth Leader Rapid Strike Force?

4. What are the characteristics of a successful Practical Growth Leader Rapid Strike Force?

5. What are the benefits and "watch-outs" of third party engagements to help you grow your business?

90-Day Adjusting Your Sails Flex Growth Plan

Time Frame	Activities

30 Days

What are your top two barriers to growth in your organization and how should you "adjust your sails" to win? What are the key components of your current dashboard? Are they the right measures reported in real time?

60 Days

What growth initiatives can you identify to assign a Rapid Strike Practical Growth Leader team to deliver against in the next 90 to 180 days?

Pilot a cross-development team focused on a critical growth initiative to learn how these entities can work successfully in your organization. What are the benefits? What are the challenges?

90 Days

Have a specific plan in progress to knock down or sail around your organization's two largest growth barriers.

Implement your comprehensive new dashboard with common objectives agreed to and embraced by the leadership team combined with real time feedback on progress versus goals.

Begin to pilot an independent outside party engagement on your top two growth initiatives that have the greatest leverage.

CHAPTER 9

Flexing All 8 Essential Steps Together

You are now ready to pull together all 8 essential steps of the Practical Growth Leader model. You have cleared 8 test hurdles and reviewed the corresponding 90-day flex plans for growth at the end of each chapter. You are now ready to review how these steps interact with each other and how they can be effectively leveraged together to win. We will now mix-up the various steps and integrate them with critical connection points. If you work toward the key connection points that integrate the concepts, you will create synergy and momentum.

Concept Connections

8 Cs of The Practical Growth Leader

If we fail to establish a culture with a passion and energy for growth, nothing else matters. The 8 Cs of the Practical Growth Leader emotionally connect with their team by laying the foundation for a true growth culture. As a review, the following 8 Cs must be effectively leveraged by the Practical Growth Leader:

1. Caring
2. Candor
3. Confronting Conflict
4. Circle of Trust
5. Collaboration
6. Credit to Others
7. Communication
8. Celebration

The bottom line is simple. You will not succeed without embracing the 8 Cs. Take the emotional leap to change your style, when necessary, in order to implement them. The decision to change, utilizing these behaviors is up to you. Remember, the biggest decisions in life are emotional. Are you ready to let go of your old style and make this transformational change? Practical Growth Leaders who are serious about changing their culture cannot afford to be observational about the 8 Cs that will build trust and reduce fear throughout your organization. Remember, fear is public enemy No. 1 in creating a growth culture. Trust is the basis of all the relationships necessary to drive growth.

Reality/Vision/Engagement Concept Connections

Employee/associate engagement does not mean anything unless you have a shared vision of the future. One of the most important things Practical Growth Leaders must do is develop a shared future vision and find new ways to communicate their consistent message over and over again.

Leaders often overestimate how well they have defined their future vision. A great test with your team is simple. Go around the table and have each member describe his or her vision for the future of the organization and write it down on a 4 x 6 card. Many leaders are often amazed at the inconsistencies that emerge among their own team. Remember, a highly engaged team going in different directions will go off the cliff faster than one that is not highly motivated. Many organizations look at engagement of employees as the fundamental measure of how their leadership team is doing. A better indicator would be a combined measurement of employee engagement as well as an understanding and commitment to the current reality and future vision of the organization.

Caring/Shared Vision Connections

The Practical Growth Leader must utilize the 8 Cs to build trust and reduce fear throughout the organization to drive growth. This is also critical to achieving a shared view of the future reality/vision. Do you really believe you can build a shared view of reality and your future vision if your people are afraid of you or do not trust your relationship with them? Leaders often fail to make this connection. The ability to create engagement and a shared view of collective reality and future vision is, in fact, directly related to your ability to emotionally connect with your people. If you fail to do this, fear levels will go up dramatically in your organization. I have heard leaders of clients in several industries say things like, "Fear can be a powerful motivator. What's wrong with having a little fear in the organization?" Let me try to answer that question. What does an organization full of fear look like? Here are some mile markers that often appear along the fear highway:

- Little or no two-way communication
- E-mails that protect our own turf and limit accountability
- A culture that wants to affix blame when anything significant goes wrong
- Few if any innovative ideas are raised to top management because of the risk of "going out on a limb"
- A general feeling that management sees employees as replaceable and interchangeable parts

Do any of these points sound familiar to you? As Dr. Phil often says, "How's that workin' for you?" If the above mile markers fit your style, chances are you are in an environment where fear is playing a significant role. The 8 Cs of the Practical Growth Leader will reduce this fear, build trust as well as engagement and enable you to gain a collective understanding and buy-in of the organization's current realities and future shared vision.

SIMPLE SQUARED Concept Connections

The Simple Squared Concept highlights group and individual leadership connections focusing on the rational as well as emotional skill sets needed to keep building on the growth side of the hill.

This Simple Squared Concept represents the diverse style and skill sets required to be a Practical Growth Leader. Are you a Hi/Low leader who can deliver a well defined strategy and also make it come alive with execution? Can you be ruthless and objective about the implications of key growth initiatives while you are also emotionally connecting with your people? Can you leverage the five percent of the total work coming across your desk that "really matters" and at the same time remain "in the moment" when you are interacting with your team members? Can you bring a big dose of passion and energy with you to work every day and at the same time collaborate carefully to discover key implications surrounding your business? Can you create emotional connections that ignite synergies across the generations? Can you do this while allowing each individual on your team the chance to leverage their unique strengths? These are critical dimensions needed to become a successful Practical Growth Leader. The Simple Squared Concept highlights the range of muscle memory required to win. If you connect with your team in both rational and emotional ways, you will build a growth culture. The Simple Squared Concept highlights the group as well as individual dimensions you need to be well-positioned to win the minds and hearts of your team.

PAC Power Growth Concept Connections

Remember, a future vision for growth is much more likely to succeed when you find PAC Power and create growth corridor intersections where you have both the customer Permission And the Capabilities to grow. The bottom line is most companies get into trouble when they stray too far away from their core capabilities. Finding the sweet spot of growth corridor intersections that are important to the customers and reflect your core capabilities are keys to sustainable growth plans.

Growth Fast Passing Zone Concept Connection Points

The PAC Power Growth Concept is made more powerful when the Growth Fast Passing Zone Concept is integrated into the consideration set. Find the sweet spot that leverages your PAC Power strengths against the competitive void or area of weakness, and you can run to daylight. Leveraging the unique strength of your organization directly against competitive voids or weaknesses will take you directly into the Fast Passing Zones.

Victory Connection Points

The key victory formula involves integrating the following elements:

- What are our core capabilities?
- Where do our customers give us permission to go?
- What are the critical elements of the buying decision?
- Where is the three-way intersection of what is critical to the customer, our key strengths and our key competitors' vulnerabilities?

By overlaying the Fast Passing Zone Growth Concept with the PAC Power Growth Concept you can create points of leverage that will create sustainable competitive advantages and real growth over time.

Peacetime Interview Connections

Where do you begin to integrate PAC Power and the Fast Passing Zone Concept? It starts with Peacetime Customer Interviews. Remember, the interviews are called peacetime because you are not trying to sell something. Many companies spend time and invest a great deal to bring solutions to the marketplace that are rated as important by the customer. That can waste a lot of time and resources. The key is to find the one or two variables that are key to the customer buying decision and focus your efforts and resources against those critical points of leverage. There is a difference between being important and being a "show stopper!"

Running with the 7 Rs Wheel Concept Connections

I get emotional when I talk about my competition. It is driven by a burning desire to win and finish first. The 7 Rs mark behaviors you can leverage when thinking about your competitors. The 7 Rs highlight the path toward victory and are listed below:

- Ruthless
- Relentless
- Respectful
- Resourceful
- Resilient
- Responsive
- Results focused

While it is critical to be focused on our competition, do not let them block a clear vision of the future. Put another way; never let your competitors rattle you and your team. If you become overly focused on your competition, it will lead to critical mistakes. That said, take any major growth initiative you are considering for your business and ask yourself a critical question. How would I feel if my competitor took this idea to my largest customer? If it wouldn't bother you, it is probably not a growth initiative that is worth pursuing going forward.

Competitive Connection Points

The strong focus on your competitor helps you discover PAC Growth

Power and Fast Passing Zones. Contingency planning against alternative competitive moves are a key part of business strategy. Leveraging your strengths against competitive weaknesses in the Fast Passing Zones while Running with the 7 Rs represents critical connection points. As highlighted earlier, it is no longer fashionable to talk about the competition. Many leaders diminish publicly the role competition plays in their consideration set. Any leader who does not acknowledge this competitive dynamic is ignorant or arrogant. The Practical Growth Leader knows that what goes on behind closed doors in strategic planning sessions paints a very different picture.

Retention Momentum Bridge Connections

All 8 essential steps to Flex Your Leadership Muscles will fail unless you find ways to keep your best people over time. Think about it. Can you think of any scenario where you will win as a leader if your best people leave you? The Retention Momentum Bridge stresses how to build trust and foster development by investing in your people. These techniques when combined with the 8 Cs of the Practical Growth Leader provide a bridge of emotional connections that leads to retention of your very best people.

While most companies talk about the need to build a retention plan, very few have solid blueprints in place to make it happen. If you adopt all the critical elements of the Retention Momentum Bridge Concept, you will build a sustainable competitive advantage over time. You can move from talking about retention as a leadership team to doing something about it by moving forward with a well orchestrated plan that can be measured over time. The top performers in your organization know they are the best people right now. They may be wondering whether or not you know they are the best. Are you ready to build the Retention Momentum Bridge? It won't be easy, but it will be worth it.

The Enemy Is Us Connection

The Dirty Dozen Reefs and Construction Zones Growth Triangle Concept featured a number of key barriers that can stall sustainable growth. These barriers live inside each of our organizations. The barriers that stop growth in your organization are actually symptoms of a culture that is not dedicated to growth. While navigating these reefs and construction zones, it is important to remember they are only symptoms of your culture problem. If you treat one individually, you are only controlling a fever rather than treating the underlying infection that is causing the illness. You must complete Step 1 effectively to transform your culture. If you fail, you are headed toward incremental, rather than breakthrough growth. Organizations have a natural inclination to add layers and levels as well as to create redundancies. These hierarchies have a tendency to slow down decision making, foster politics, create redundancies and promote silo behavior. Flattening the organization levels will uncover these root causes for stalling growth. A flatter organization is also far more likely to consider the "big picture" with regard to what is in the best interest of the entire business entity, rather than individual communities within the organization. If you view additional layers and management positions with a critical and skeptical eye, you are far more likely to be a successful Practical Growth Leader.

At the end of the day, it is the integration of the individual steps of The Practical Growth Leader model that causes you to quickly gain momentum driving change in your organization. Each of the 8 steps becomes even more powerful when they are interlocking, rather than stand alone concepts. The model points out that the Practical Growth Leader will win when you focus on five things:

1. Lead your clients and customers
2. Drive business growth throughout your organization
3. Treat your people well
4. Focus externally toward the marketplace
5. Find critical strategic points of leverage that align your strengths, competitive weaknesses and the most critical variables to your customers' or clients' buying decision.

What's Next?

Practical Growth Leaders must sustain momentum. We will now transition to a roadmap for sustaining the powerful momentum you and your team have created. It is not enough to implement the model and move forward. How will you build momentum throughout the organization? How will you protect your new strategic choices during times of change and leadership turnover? Everything starts with a resilient Practical Growth Leader and the process never ends. You must bring the model to life every day through leadership by example. You must celebrate the desired accomplishments, behaviors and actions that will drive business growth. This will not be an easy task. The fires that have to be put out every day will still be there when you go to work in the morning. How will you respond to the challenge?

CHAPTER 10

How Do You Sustain Flexing Your Leadership Muscles Every Day?

Creating Muscle Memory

The Eagles, the talented California rock group from the 1970s recorded a song called "The Long Run." Don Henley sings, "Who can go the distance? We'll find out in the long run." Will you be able to develop the muscle memory to go the distance? The biggest single "long run" challenge you will encounter is developing the muscle memory to keep moving toward implementing the steps of the Grow Now Model. The fact is we are all victims of our own habits and behaviors. It will be very easy to fall back into the usual patterns of your leadership style. We all tend to quietly gravitate back to our comfort zone. In addition, the inertia of most of our organizations will reinforce our old behaviors. Are you going to circulate to emotionally connect with your front-line troops or retreat back into your office in front of a computer screen to respond to the 85 e-mails you received in the last 24 hours? Are you going to gain original customer insights by conducting Peacetime Interviews or simply go back to market and sell as you always have to your customers? Are you willing to spend more time looking for key trends and competitive activity in your business? Will you build a solid Retention Momentum Bridge in the organization to retain your best employees? Are you going to help lead the culture transformation required to achieve growth?

There are several tools to help you develop the 8 step muscle memory you need to win. These building materials involve things you do, in fact, control:

- Log book
- Personal Journal
- 90-Day Flex Plans
- Leadership Team Buy-in

Log Book

Keep an ongoing log book that records how you and your team spend your time together. Are you focusing on what matters to really address the changes needed to transform your culture? How much time are you and your team spending on culture transformation, customer insights, finding PAC Power, talking about Fast Passing Zones, building the Retention Momentum Bridge and sailing around the growth reefs as well as construction zones? If you have not changed how you are currently spending at least 50 percent of your time, you will revert back to your comfort zone. The log is a quantitative way to measure how you and your team are spending your time differently as a result of the 8 steps.

Personal Journal

Many successful presidents from Abraham Lincoln to Ronald Reagan have utilized personal diaries or journals. Remember, leading change is a full-contact sport. There will be many difficult and discouraging days ahead. However, if you keep a record of your personal leadership journey, it will serve as a source of inspiration during the tough times. I kept a personal journal of my professional leadership journey over the past 30 years. It has often been an inspirational and reinforcing strength that I have drawn on to make tough decisions and make a choice to go a different direction. It will also help you keep track of your career story as it unfolds over several decades.

90-Day Flex Plans for Growth

The reason we put the 90-Day Flex Plan for Growth at the end of each of the 8 steps is to provide a blueprint for jumpstarting your momentum. It's important that you keep changes at a minimum – don't change everything at once. The 90-Day Flex Plans for Growth provide a roadmap for how to begin the change that is needed to win. You have to break the activities into manageable chunks. Overlay the various 90-Day Flex Plans for Growth against your organization's priorities and begin to take the first steps toward leading change. Don't try to do it all at once. Remember, this journey will take time and patience. But the transformation you witness will make all the hard work worthwhile.

Leadership Team Buy-in

You must secure the buy-in and commitment of your leadership team. You cannot win without them. Their enthusiasm begins with a top-down commitment to pursue sustainable growth as the No. 1 priority of the organization. If your team believes that, "This too will pass," then you are in serious trouble. The commitment to growth must have multiple-year incentives that directly impact your leaders' compensation and performance evaluations. In addition, you must identify those who will not buy-in to the new vision and terminate their relationship with your organization. These terminations will also send a clear signal to the rest of your organization about your commitment to transforming your culture.

What's Next?

The very first thing to do is to identify some "low hanging fruit" and aggressively go after these opportunities to get some quick, early victories with short cycle times. As the number of team victories pile up, the confidence of the organization will grow. Don Shula, the former coach of the Miami Dolphins, had a team that achieved the only undefeated NFL record in history (17-0 in 1972). Imagine how the confidence level of that Dolphins team grew every week as the team momentum continued to grow. Winning consistently builds confidence and trust in your team members. You should always try to win early and often. Even small wins on a 90-day cycle can set the momentum wheels in motion for bigger wins later.

Sustain Flexing Your Grow Now Leadership Muscles

How do you sustain the momentum needed to keep flexing your Grow Now Leadership Muscles? Why is it that most organizations fail to sustain the change needed to create a growth culture? We already outlined the challenges and tools that can be utilized to develop a Practical Growth Leader muscle memory. There are some more hazards that must be avoided to sustain the momentum going forward.

Sustainability Sand Traps

There are sustainability sand traps that must be avoided by the Practical Growth Leader. These hazards will reduce your momentum and cause the organization to reject the Grow Now Model:

1. Top down commitment wavers over time.
2. Turnover in key leadership positions.
3. Early growth initiatives result in big losses.
4. There are no consequences if leaders fail to embrace the model.
5. Top leaders set growth objectives so high that they are unrealistic and lack credibility.

Let's look at these five sustainability sand traps and how to address each of them.

Top-Down Commitment

If the organization senses any wavering on the commitment of the top leaders of the organization to transform into a growth culture, momentum will soon be gone from your team. Practical Growth Leaders must never give anyone the sense that they are backing away from the 8 essential steps to flex their leadership muscles. In fact, it is really important that you reinforce your commitment to leading a growth culture during the tough times. Reach out and emotionally connect with your team about the commitment to overcome adversity and win the race.

Turnover of Key Growth Leaders

If you lose the best leaders in your organization, your growth momentum will grind to a screeching halt. Your key leaders are the linchpins to leading transformational change. It is highly unlikely that your second team collectively is up to the task. That is why the Retention Momentum Bridge is so important as a part of the Practical Growth Leader tool box. Retention begins with your very best leaders. They are looked up to by the rest of the organization and counted on by your front-line associates to successfully guide the transformation of the culture. If they leave, your organization will lose confidence and you will lose momentum. Winning begins with keeping your very best leaders solidly beside you every step of the way.

Early Substantial Losses

Nothing will cause an organization to lose confidence in leadership faster than a few, quick losses that have a substantial negative impact on your top and bottom line. Be sure when you pick the top three growth initiatives that you plan to launch first into the marketplace, that you screen them to make sure that the early ones have a high probability of success. Avoid coming out of the gate with your highest risk growth initiatives early. Also, make sure that you manage your risk carefully by testing small and scaling fast to reduce the likelihood of heavy upfront capital investments in growth initiatives that prove to be unsuccessful and erode profitability.

No Consequences

The leaders of your organization must understand that there are specific consequences if they fail to embrace the changes needed to sustain growth. This unity is also important for your leaders to accept a specific time-frame, during which they must embrace any changes that will assure success. If they do not accept this premise, we will move on without them. This tough love is one of the most difficult parts of being a Practical Growth Leader, and is also one of the most critical to the long term success of your organization.

Realistic and Attainable Objectives

One of the fastest ways to derail Practical Growth Leader momentum is to assign growth objectives to your organization that are not realistic or attainable. When this happens, the change leadership initiatives lose both credibility and steam. This places a dark cloud over your growth initiatives and optimism is replaced by distrust and cynicism. Your organization's growth objectives must be credible and have buy-in from your leadership team.

Practical Growth Leader – "Grow Now"

Consistency should provide the foundation for your personal leadership brand. People like predictable and consistent leaders. They want to know and trust that your responses to key situations will be predictable and consistent which reduces their uncertainty in dealing with their leaders every day. A Practical Growth Leader who behaves inconsistently in key situations will frustrate their people and experience high turnover as they leave for greener pastures. The most important thing you can do as a Practical Growth Leader is to behave in a consistent and predictable way. Consistency can be the difference between winning or losing the trust, as well as confidence, of your team.

Be Yourself

We have reviewed a number of concepts in the 8 steps to flex your Practical Leadership Muscles. It is critical that you apply these steps in a way that is consistent with who you really are and how others see you every day. No one responds favorably to a leader who is trying to be someone else. That is usually not seen in a positive way by those who follow your lead. Apply these 8 Practical Growth Leader steps in ways that you are comfortable with inside your existing leadership style.

You have read about many of my personal stories related to leadership. Keep a personal journal of your stories. They represent key and unique aspects of your personal leadership style that you can draw on during the tough times. The bottom line is to be yourself while you lead your customers and clients, grow your business and treat your people well.

Remember that your people are looking for a predictable, consistent and trusted leader every day. The last thing most of your team members want or need is for you to be their personal friend.

The secret to being a strong Practical Growth Leader is to thread the needle of professionalism in an engaging, motivating and caring fashion that your people will respond to, while not crossing the line into the friendship zone. I have managed other leaders who became my friends over time. However, during our business experience together, I have always been extremely careful to draw very clear lines to avoid mixing leadership with friendship. You must do this to avoid a conflict of interest and to be viewed as a consistent and equitable leader among all of your team members.

The Final Frontier – The World Around You

Captain James T. Kirk, played by William Shatner, introduced every episode of the cult television series "Star Trek," with the same words: "Space... the Final Frontier." You have reached the "Final Frontier" of Grow Now. Remember, the world is changing around us faster than ever before. "Be in the moment" every day and observe these changes. The pace of change is accelerating rapidly. The playbook that used to evolve over a period of years is now becoming outdated in months, weeks, days and even hours. Companies that learn how to assimilate data into a story and convert it quickly into major sustainable growth initiatives with immediate action plans will leave their competitors in the starting blocks. Speed to market, based on new learning every day is the key to being the pace car in the growth race.

There are many companies who know what to do. They just don't know how to leverage speed to do it faster than anyone else. Focus on raising the sense of urgency in your organization to be decisive and move quickly. This is the definition of playing to win. I would much rather create a team that can make and implement a decision too quickly (even if it is wrong), than a leadership team that is consistently too slow to make the call. That team never catches up to its competition.

Success begins by paying close attention to the world around you. What is happening in best-practice companies? What are the key trends in other industries? How are the customer segments changing? The answers to these questions are evolving at an ever increasing rate. Practical Growth Leaders who are successful know they must continually adjust their play books to adjust to these changes.

Circle of the Practical Growth Leader

Remember the connections of the concepts reviewed in each of the 8 steps. Build a circle of growth around these concepts to create a 360 degree culture transformation in your organization. The circle of the Practical Growth Leader provides the integrated roadmap to effectively lead your team toward victory.

Concept 10.1

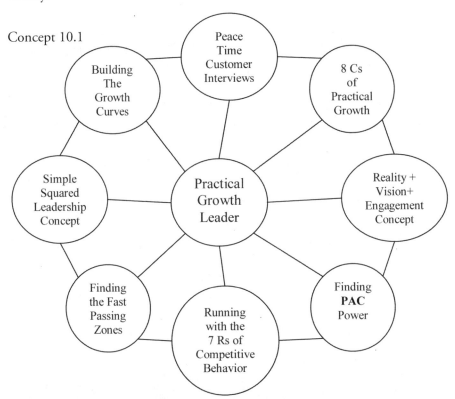

Circle of Practical Growth Integration Concept

Final Thoughts

Are you ready to Grow Now and move forward with the 8 essential steps to Flex Your Leadership Muscles? You have cleared all the hurdles and flex plans; the rest is up to you. Remember, the biggest decisions in life are emotional. The decision to get married. The decision to have kids. The decision to join or leave a company. I would contend that the decision to become a true Practical Growth Leader is also an emotional one.

Many of the techniques outlined in this book will not only make you more successful as an individual leader, they will also put you in the right place at the right time to put points on the scoreboard. Bud Frankel, founder of Frankel & Co. Promotion Agency in Chicago, once told me while we were riding in a car together many years ago: "It is one thing to be at the right place at the right time. It is something special to be at the right place at the right time and know it!" My question to you is simple: "Do you know it?" The emotional decision to transform your leadership style is yours to make going forward. You have the tools, the playbook, the roadmap and the insights to make it happen. Do you have the will to force yourself out of your comfort zone to do it? The rest is up to you.

The Rolling Stones hit "Start Me Up," kicked off our journey to become Practical Growth Leaders. I would like to end with another memorable Rolling Stones song, "You Can't Always Get What You Want." Mick Jagger purrs, "You can't always get what you want... but if you try sometimes, you just might find... you get what you need!" Being a Practical Growth Leader every day is what your team and entire organization needs. It is what your clients and/or customers need. It will be a difficult journey full of challenges, but it will also be a rewarding one full of unlimited possibilities. As Mr. Spock, (played by Leonard Nimoy), from "Star Trek," would often say, "Live Long and Prosper." You are now ready to engage, motivate and guide your team to grow - every day!

About the Authors

Jim Welch

As president and founder of "The Growth Leader, Inc.", Jim is a member of Five Star Speakers. Jim is also a principal owner in "LEADERFUELNOW, LLC," a company dedicated to fueling high octane business results. He works with Fortune 500 clients and entrepreneurial organizations from coast to coast. As a former Senior Vice-President of Marketing with Hallmark, Welch brings over 25 years of leadership passion, hands on experience and a winning track record to get top line and bottom line results. Welch is THE Practical Growth Leader whose 8-step program has achieved real world results for a quarter of a century.

Welch and his wife, Christine, live in Overland Park, Kansas. They have two sons, Jeff, a senior at the University of Kansas and Mike, a sophomore who also attends Kansas University.

Bill Althaus

Bill Althaus is an award-winning member of *The Examiner's* sports staff. Althaus won the Docking Award signifying the Kansas City Media Personality of the Year in 2006 and followed that up by winning the Morris Communications Excellence in Journalism Award in 2007. He has been honored by United Press International, the Associated Press and the Missouri Press Association. Althaus has authored books on NFL superstars Priest Holmes, Dante Hall and longtime Kansas City Chiefs bandleader and community icon Tony DiPardo and has a new book on the history of the Chiefs arriving on bookstands in the fall of 2007.

Althaus and his wife Stacy live in Grain Valley, Missouri. They have two sons, Zach, a senior at Rockhurst University, and Sean, a sophomore at Blue

To book Jim Welch
to speak at your next
event, please contact

Jim Welch
The Growth Leader, Inc.
www.thegrowthleader.com

Jim Welch is represented by PowerHouse.
Visit www.powerhousenow.com

Book Notes

Introduction

1. Jerry Seinfeld Quotes and Trivia at Filmspot, www.filmspot.com, people5005/jerryseinfeld/trivia.html-35K-June 8,2007

2. "It's What You Learn After You Know Everything That Counts" Inspiring Quotes, www.fireflycoaching.com

3. "Field of Dreams" (1989) – Memorable Quotes Earths Biggest Movie Database TM

4. "Are You Ready for some Hank" www.usatoday.com2002-09-05Williams-xhtm-57k-

5. Quote Details: Oprah Winfrey: Whatever you fear most... - The ... www.quotationspage.com/quote/31081.html

6. Vince Lombardi Quotes www.brainyquote.com/quotes/quotes/v/vincelomb1 1546 7.html

7. Zig Ziglar Quotes 2 – Self help author www.woopidoo.com/business_quotes/authors/zigziglarplanning-quotes.htm-26K-

8. The Movie Wavs Page "Back To The Future" Wavs MVP MovieQuotes, www.moviewavs.com/movies/BackToTheFuture.html

Chapter 1

1. Start Me Up – www.Keno.org/stores_lyrics/StartMeUp.html-5K-

2. "From White Out to Medicine" – Campus News www.utahstatesman.com/news/2005/04/01/campusnews/from-whiteouttomedicine-909973.shtml-39K

3. YouTube - Wikipedia, the free encyclopedia wikipedia.org/wiki/YouTube-172K

4. George Costanza – www.adrianspeyer.com/george.htm-38K

5. "Behold the Turtle: 5 Ways to Effect Positive Change" by Kevin Wheeler 2004, Global Learning Resources, Inc. www.giresources.com/articles_view.php?id=180-18K

6. I Still Haven't Found What I'm Looking For (The Joshua Tree) lyrics. interference.com/U2/lyrics/albums/Joshua-tree/i-still-havent-found-what.html.10K

7. Joe Montana Was the Comeback King espn.go.com/sportscentury/features/00016306.html-19K

8. Lincoln on Leadership CoachThee.comhome.att.net/coachthee/Archives/Lincoln.html-72K

9. "Greed is Good" American Rhetoric Movie Speech "Wall Street" (1987) www.americanrhetoric.com/MovieSpeechwallstreet.html-17K

10. Magical Disney Forums: Pirates of the Caribbean At Worlds End www.magicalmountain.net/forums/form_posts.asp?TID=15918PID=17850-41K-

11. Roger Ebert Quotes Thinkexist.com "Finding Quotes Was Never-This Easy"-thinkexist.com/quotes/roger_ebert/-30K-

12. Mary Kay Ash Quotes www.brainyquote.com/quotes/authors/m/marykayash173353.html-15K-

13. Business Summaries - Never Eat Alone www.bizsum.com/2page/b_NeverEatAlone.php - 22k

14. John Lennon ezinearticles.com/?Life-Is-What-Happens-When-You-Are-Busy-Making-Other-Plansid=553076-28K

15. *Chicago Tribune* Legends of the Bowl January 30, 2007 http://www.chicagotribune.com/sports/football

16. Tony Blair Quotes www.quotationspage.com/quote/39841.html

17. American National Business Hall of Fame, ANBHF Mary Kay Ash www.anbhf.org/laureates/mkash.html

18. Why You Should collect Shatnerisms whyyoushould.org/collect/Shatnerisms

19. Jaws (1975) - Memorable quotes www.imdb.com/title/tt0073195/quotes

20. William James Quotes thinkexist.com/quotation/whenever_you-re_in_conflict_with_someone-there_is/227935.html

21. Dr. Maya Angelou - Andi's Quotes: Part 39 www.andilipman.com/quotes39.html - 36k

22. Meet The Parents - www.meettheparents.com

23. Paul McCartney Quotes thinkexist.com/quotes/paul_mccartney/ - 33k

24. The O'Jays Lyrics - Love Train Lyrics www.stlyrics.com/lyrics/undercoverbrother/lovetrain.htm - 5k

25. Super Millionaire - Regis Philbin - Who Wants To Be A Millionaire ... www.realitytvworld.com/supermillionaire/ - 82k

26. List of The Dick Van Dyke Show episodes - Wikipedia, the free ... en.wikipedia.org/wiki/List_of_The_Dick_Van_Dyke_Show_episodes - 65k

27. Seinfeld - Official Site www.sonypictures.com/tv/shows/seinfeld

28. Norman Schwarzkopf Quotes – United States Army General www.quotemonk.com/authors/norman-schwarzkopf/index.htm

29. Harry Truman www.wow4U.com

30. George Brett Quotes www.baseball-almanac.com/quotes/quobrett.
shtml - 26k

31. Simon and Garfunkel – "Like a Bridge Over Troubled Water" Lyrics
www.lyricsfreak.com/s/simon+and+garfunkel/bridge+over+troubled+water_
20124580.html

32. Dolly Parton-Quotations from great song lyrics, song quotes www.
corsinet.com/braincandy/miscsong.html - 69k

33. Confucius - The connection between learning and doing www.psy.
gla.ac.uk/~steve/best/activism.html - 4k

34. Martin Luther King, Jr. usinfo.state.gov/usa/infousa/facts/democ-
rac/38.htm - 14k

35. John F. Kennedy Definition and much more from answers.com
www.answers.com/topic/john-f-kennedy - 588k

36. Winston Churchill www.anglik.net/churchill.htm - 17k

37. Ronald Reagan – Tear Down This Wall www.reaganfoundation.
org/reagan/speeches/wall.asp - 24k

38. *In Search Of Excellence,* Tom Peters and Robert Waterman www.
businessballs.com/tompetersinsearchofexcellence.htm - 11k

39. *Learning to Lead With Fertilizer and a Watering Can* - Knowledge ...
knowledge.wharton.upenn.edu/article.cfm?articleid=8 - 36k

40. Oprah Winfrey Quotes www.brainyquote.com/quotes/quotes/o/
oprahwinfr103803.html

Chapter 2

1. Dr. Maya Angelou dvsshop.ca/dvcafe/madscreen/theatricquotes.htm-
12K

2. Leland McKensie www.imdb.com/title/tt0090466/quotes-26K

3. Quotes about Leadership – Tom Peters www.cornerstonesofleadership.
com/quotes-leadership.htm - 20k

4. Ralph Waldo Emerson www.wisdomquotes.com/002418.html-10K

5. Gallup www.idspackaging.com/common/paper_18/
Trust%20Or%20Bust.htm-21K

6. Goodfellas 1990 Memorable Quotes www.imdv.com/title/
tt0099685/quotes-57K

7. "Stairway to Heaven" Lyrics www.brave.com/bollyrics/stairhea.htm-4K

8. E-mail received from Ron Cox, ACE Hardware retailer from Appleton
Wisconsin following my speech at the Midwest Hardware Association delivered on 2/12/07.

9. "The A Team" (1983) Memorable Quotes www.imdb.com/title/tt0084967I-45K

10. Winston Churchill Quotes www.thinkexist.com/quotation/attitude_is_a_little_thing_that_makes_a_big/219106html-34K-

11. Millennial Generation Beloit College www.deltachiconvention.org/handouts/handouts/Millennial_Genpdf

12. Cross Generational Communication – Implications in the Work Environment, Office of Institutional Equity Duke University

Chapter 3

1. Peter F. Drucker Quotes www.thinkexist.com/quotation/a_business_exits_to_create_a/164288html-32K

2. BIG Research study for the National Retail Federation, Consumer/Beyond Civil Service, "The Seattle Times", Sunday March 25, 2007

3. Bill Althaus personal interview conducted with Tim and Steve Pace in Independence Missouri "Where the Customer is Treated Like Family."

4. Cheers Theme Song Lyrics "Where Everybody Knows Your Name" www.lyricsondemand.com/tvthemes/cheerslyrics.html-11K

5. iNTouch Success Center providing real time customer feedback

6. Hill, Charles, Jones, Gareth. "Southwest Airlines Low Cost Structure" Strategic Management Theory – An Integrated Approach (pg. 89)

7. Jim Welch personal interview with Roy Spence, President GSD&M, Austin, Texas regarding permanent display of Agency Values (August, 2004)

8. Brand Channel.com/education_glossary.asp-54K

9. "Knute Rockne All American" 1940 www.imdb.com/title/tt0032676/-41K

10. Bob Dylan: "The Times They Are A-Changin'" www.bobdylan.com/albums/times.html-6K

11. Ray Kroc Woopidoo Business Success – Motivational Business Quotes www.woopidoo.com/-38K

12. The Office: The Dundies – TV Squad www.tvsquad.com/2005/09/20/the-office-the-dundies/-66K

13. Amazon.com: "The Candidate": DVD: Robert Redford,Peter Boyle,Melvyn ... www.amazon.com/Candidate-Robert-Redford/dp/6304696507 - 147k

14. Bill Gates Quotes www.thinkexist.com/quotation/your_most_un-happy_customers_are_your_greatest/147304.html-33K

15. Roger Staubach Quotes www.brainyquote.com/quotes/authors/r/roger_staubachhtml-18K

16. Sam Walton Biography – Fresh Thinking Business www.freshthinkingbusiness.com/sam-walton.html-19K

17. Marshall Field & Co. Business People – United States Biography www.kipnotes.com/RetailDepartmentstores.html-116K

18. 50+Free Customer Service Quotes – Kate Zabriskie www.businesstrainingworks.com/Onsite%20Training20%Web/Free%20Articles/02%20customer%20%Service20%Quotes.html-27K

Chapter 4

1. Quote Details: Steve Jobs: Innovation distinguishes between a ... www. quotationspage.com/quote/38349.html - 9k

2. Staying on Target Article - *The Wall Street Journal* – Monday, May 7, 2007

3. Knute Rockne www.rare-football-books.com/ - 28k

4. Ronald Reagan Quotes www.brainyquote.com/quotes/quotes/r/ronaldreag147706.html - 26k

5. Quotations by General George S. Patton www.generalpatton.com/quotes.html - 13k

6. Office Space (1999) www.imdb.com/title/tt0151804/ - 46k

7. Winston Churchill Quotes www.brainyquote.com/quotes/quotes/w/winstonchu104164.html - 31k

8. Internet Changes Everything: baby boomer financial services www.ladlass.com/ice/archives/011138.html - 72k

9. Who Are 50-UPers? The boomer senior market www.50upexpo.com/market-facts.htm - 29k

10. "Helicopter" Parents Appear to Defy Socioeconomic Pegging – Article – USA Today April 4, 2007

11. Jim Welch conducted a personal interview with Jonathan Pontell – generations expert – in Orange County, CA in May 2007 regarding Generation Jones

12. 1984 (television commercial) - Wikipedia, the free encyclopedia en.wikipedia.org/wiki/1984_(television_commercial) - 46k

13. "Women as Chief Purchasing Officers for their Families" - *Business Week* Article – Monday February 14, 2005

14. Women living alone - America's Families and Living Arrangements: 2003 www.census.gov/prod/2004pubs/p20-553.pdf

15. ABC News: Excerpt: 'The Female Brain' abcnews.go.com/GMA/Books/story?id=2274147&page=1

16. Women still outlive men by an average of five years - "USA Today" Article - June 12, 2006

17. BrandWeek – Marti Barletta – September 4, 2006

18. Women Traveling Solo Article - Solo, So Well – The Kansas City Star – Sunday, April 15, 2007

19. Neil Armstrong quotes thinkexist.com/quotes/neil_armstrong/ - 30k

20. "Golden Earrings" - Radar Love Lyrics for Song www.stlyrics.com/songs/g/goldenearrings8922/radarlove301959.html - 8k

Chapter 5

1. WarGames (1983) - Memorable quotes www.imdb.com/title/tt0086567/quotes - 38k

2. Bruce Springsteen | "Born To Run" lyrics www.lyricsfreak.com/b/bruce+springsteen/born+to+run_20025020.html - 17k

3. Queen | "Another One Bites The Dust" lyrics www.lyricsfreak.com/q/queen/another+one+bites+the+dust_20112678.html - 17k

4. "Hill Street Blues" (1981) - Memorable quotes www.imdb.com/title/tt0081873/quotes - 34k

5. Tony Soprano on Management | Quotes www.tonysopranoonmanagement.com/quotes.html - 17k

6. "Patton" (1970) - Movie Info - Yahoo! Movies movies.yahoo.com/movie/1800105199/info - 38k

7. "Forrest Gump" (1994) - Memorable quotes www.imdb.com/title/tt0109830/quotes - 52k

8. "Jerry Maguire"(1996) - Memorable quotes www.imdb.com/title/tt0116695/quotes - 44k

9. Right Guard - 1 Ages: Old enough to know better. (because the game has been www.fundexgames.com/instructions/pdf/AdVersity_3872.pdf

10. "Apocalypse Now" (1979) - Memorable quotes www.imdb.com/title/tt0078788/quotes - 48k

11. Willie Nelson – "On the Road Again" Lyrics www.cowboylyrics.com/lyrics/nelson-willie/on-the-road-again-2509.html - 17k

Chapter 6

1. snopes.com: Tony Blair quote msgboard.snopes.com/message/ultimatebb.php?/ubb/get_topic/f/32/t/000459/p/1.html - 96k

2. Warren Buffett Quotes www.brainyquote.com/quotes/authors/w/warren_buffett.html - 21k

3. Quote Details: Lee Iacocca: The speed of the... - The Quotations Page www.quotationspage.com/quote/8574.html - 9k

Chapter 7

1. Oliver Wendell Holmes - The greatest thing in this world is not so much where we are, but ... www.quotedb.com/quotes/1523 - 14k

2. Dell Home & Home Office   www.dell.com/us/en/dhs/default.htm - 46k

3. Pepsi Slogan, Kentucky Fried Chicken slogan, Translation Funnies www.ojohaven.com/fun/translation.funnies.html - 26k

4. Rolls Royce Car Translations that are Marketing Mistakes www.i18nguy.com/translations.html - 67k

5. Swiffer Product Women in Italy Like To Clean but Shun The Quick and Easy - WSJ.com   online.wsj.com/article/SB114593112611534922.html

6. Reverse Mentoring – "Kansas City Star" Article "Sharing Bridges Generation Gap" - June 12, 2007

7. Starbucks Going Green - "Brand Week" Article – June 22, 2007

8. TIVO/DVR increased use - It all "adds" up: TV commercials of the future: "with pressure ... findarticles.com/p/articles/mi_m1272/is_2702_132/ai_110531037 - 33k

9. Walgreens hits 4000: goal is 7000 stores by 2010 "Drug Store News"... findarticles.com/p/articles/mi_m3374/is_4_25/ai_99309228 - 30k

10. *Business Week* Article - BW Online | October 6, 2003 | Is Wal-Mart Too Powerful?   www.businessweek.com/magazine/content/03_40/b3852001_mz001.htm - 75k - Jun 24, 2007

11. Online Extra: Skinner's Winning McDonald's Recipe www.businessweek.com/magazine/content/07_06/b4020007.htm - 64k - Jun 24, 2007

12. Starbucks - Bloomberg.com: Worldwide www.bloomberg.com/apps/news?pid=20601087&sid=avPM3DpuUMik&refer=home - Jun 24, 2007

13. Procter & Gamble - Swifferwww.dcontinuum.com/content/portfolio/1/89/ - 9k

14. THE BEATLES - HELP! LYRICS www.sing365.com/music/Lyric.nsf/Help-lyrics-The-Beatles/94A50592CE91D51248256BC2001356C4 - 10k

Chapter 8

1. Outdoors Forum - messages #104689 .1 community.netscape.com/n/pfx/forum.aspx?tsn=1&nav=messages&webtag=ws-outdoors&tid=104689 - 59k

2. Dolly Parton quotes   thinkexist.com/quotation/we_cannot_direct_ the_ wind-but_we_can_adjust_the/203584.html - 32k

3. Walt Disney World Resort   disneyworld.disney.go.com/ - 66k

4. *The Chronicle:* 5/25/2001: Pearls of Wisdom From Jon Bon Jovi chronicle.com/weekly/v47/i37/37a01002.htm - 15k

5. Zig Ziglar Quotes 2 – Self help author www.woopidoo.com/business_quotes/authors/zigziglarplanning-quotes.htm-26K-

6. famous David Ogilvy quotes -ThinkExist www.thinkexist.com/English/Author/x/Author_4793_1.htm - 24k

Chapter 9

1. Thoughts from Dr. Phil- Works and Words www.worksandwords. com/phil.htm - 5k

Chapter 10

1. Eagles – "The Long Run" Lyrics www.lyrics007.com/ Eagles%20Lyrics/The%20Long%20Run%20Lyrics.html - 16k

2. "Perfect Season" - Wikipedia, the free encyclopedia en.wikipedia.org/wiki/Perfect_Season - 33k

3. "Star Trek V: The Final Frontier"- Wikipedia, the free encyclopedia en.wikipedia.org/wiki/Star_Trek_V:_The_Final_Frontier - 60k

4. Personal Conversation with Bud Frankel, Founder of Frankel & Co. Promotion Agency, Chicago, IL

5. THE ROLLING STONES lyrics – "You Can't Always Get What You Want" www.oldielyrics.com/lyrics/the_rolling_stones/you_cant_always_get_ what_you_want.html - 6k

6. Spock - Wikipedia, the free encyclopedia en.wikipedia.org/wiki/ Spock - 76k

Index